Shine On!

30 Biblical Principles for Radiant Living

Deborah Presnell

GRACE
PUBLISHING

BROKEN ARROW, OK

Unless otherwise noted, Scripture verses used in this study are taken from the New American Standard Bible. Copyright © 1960, 1962, 1963, 1968, 1971, 1972, 1973, 1975, 1977, 1995 by The Lockman Foundation.

Scripture quotations marked CEB are taken from the Common English Bible. Copyright © 2011 Church Resources Development Corp.

Scripture quotations marked ESV are taken from *The Holy Bible, English Standard Version*. Copyright © 2001 by Crossway Bibles, a division of Good News Publishers.

Scripture quotations marked KJV are taken from Kings James Version of the Bible.

Scripture quotations marked NKJV taken from the *New King James Version*®. Copyright © 1982 by Thomas Nelson. Used by permission. All rights reserved.

Scripture quotations marked NIV are taken from THE HOLY BIBLE, NEW INTERNATIONAL VERSION®, NIV® Copyright © 1973, 1978, 1984, 2011 by Biblica, Inc.® Used by permission. All rights reserved worldwide.

Scripture quotations marked RSV are taken from the Revised Standard Version of the Bible, copyright © 1946, 1952, and 1971 the Division of Christian Education of the National Council of the Churches of Christ in the United States of America. Used by permission. All rights reserved.

With the exception of brief quotations embodied in a review, this book or parts thereof may not be reproduced in any form without permission. Photocopying, scanning, uploading, and/or distribution of this book via the Internet or any other means without written permission of the publisher is illegal.

For Information Contact
Grace Publishing
PO Box 1233
Broken Arrow, OK 74013

Cover Image: Depositphotos

Shine On! 30 Biblical Principles for Radiant Living

ISBN 13: 978-1-60495-063-2

Copyright © 2020 by Deborah Presnell. Published by Grace Publishing House, Broken Arrow, Oklahoma. All rights reserved.

About Copyrights

First Timothy 5:17-18 instructs us to give the laborer his wages, specifically those who labor in the Word and doctrine. Even so, some people who would never shoplift may think nothing of copying a book. The results are the same; it's theft.

As Christians, we have a moral, as well as a legal, responsibility to see that authors receive fair compensation for their efforts. Many of them depend on the income from the sale of their books as their livelihood, as do the artists, editors, and numerous other people who work to make their books available to you.

With the exception of brief quotations embodied in a review, this book, or parts thereof may not be reproduced in any form without permission. It is protected by copyright and is not intended to be shared with or duplicated by others who have not purchased it for themselves from authorized sellers. Photocopying, scanning, uploading, and/or distribution of this book via the Internet or any other means without written permission of the publisher is illegal and punishable by law.

If you have a copy of this book that was not purchased by or for you, please be aware that you are using an illegal, pirated copy. Please purchase only authorized editions, from authorized sellers, and do not participate in or encourage piracy of copyrighted materials.

Your support of the author's rights is appreciated.

Dedication

I dedicate this Bible study to Yvonne Lehman for patiently teaching me how to put my words into proper writing format. You are a special mentor.

~ ~ ~

I also dedicate this book to my son, Will, who gave me countless stories, most of which, moved me to a greater understanding of God. Grinding play sand into a gallon-sized container of peanut butter, however, provided absolutely no spiritual lesson — except to prepare me for what lies ahead.

*Don't shine so others can see you.
Shine so that through you, others can see Him.*

C. S. Lewis
Author, Theologian and Christian Apologist

How to Use This Study

Shine On! is designed to be used alone or with a small group. In addition to this book, you'll need a Bible and a pen/pencil. Scriptures primarily come from the *New American Standard Bible* (NASB), but when another version is used, it's noted. It is important to keep in mind as you study that when a Bible version capitalizes the entire word LORD, it is reflecting the Hebrew term *Yahweh* — the eternal I Am (from a root word meaning "to be," or eternal existence). When the word *Lord* is written with standard capitalization, it is personal, reflecting the Hebrew word *Adonai*, literally meaning "my Lord," (from a root word which suggests sovereignty, strength and power).[1]

The time you spend in each chapter will vary. You can complete a chapter in one sitting or complete it over several days.

I encourage you to pray before beginning each study. Ask God to reveal what He wants you to see and learn. Be honest with God and yourself.

At the end of each chapter, there is space to journal your thoughts under *What Meant the Most to You from Today's Study*. Also, at the end, you will find suggested *Applications* to extend the study and put what you've learned into practice. Finally, *Light from the Scriptures* are beautiful passages from God's Word. Some may align with the study of the current chapter, but most don't. They're meant, instead, to draw attention to God's character, bring Him praise, or be used as a prayer to say back to God.

You're embarking on a life-changing journey. Shine on!

Introduction

How do we shine?

Rosemary walked into my office with defeat written on her face. "How do you do it?" she asked.

Rosemary had a troubled background. Her house had burned down, resulting in the death of her small child, and a series of boyfriends had left her confused. Physical, emotional, and substance abuse was a way of life.

"How are you so happy? You always have a smile on your face, even when I think you may have been crying. How can you be so joyful?"

I smiled.

"Oh, I have troubles. Life is definitely not easy. But I wouldn't walk out the door each day without God."

Rosemary was searching, and God had been preparing her heart for this moment. I shared the source of my strength and how I depend on God to help me with every aspect of my life. Rosemary wanted the same God in her life. She longed for a new start. Two hours later, Rosemary prayed to receive Jesus Christ as her Savior.

Five years later, Rosemary knocked on my half-open door, then stepped into my office for a surprise visit. Radiance shown on her face as she declared, "This is the place — the place where I met Jesus and my life was changed forever."

That's what we're told in Psalm 34:5. ***Those who look to [God] are radiant!*** (NIV). We radiate our faith, His strength, our hope, and *explainable* joy.

Like Rosemary, we shine when we walk closely with God and depend on Him to meet our needs: physical, social, emotional, and mental. Spending time in God's Word matures us.

The primary focus of *Shine On! 30 Biblical Principles for Radiant Living* is how to use biblical principles to nurture our relationship with Jesus Christ, live victoriously despite circumstances, and shine in a dark world.

Jesus tells us this in Matthew 5:16: *"Let your light shine before men in such a way that they may see your good works, and glorify your Father who is in heaven."*

Table of Contents

1. We Are Who God Says We Are 11
2. Listening to God 20
3. Darkened with Disappointment 27
4. Loving People in a Diverse Culture 36
5. Actions Speak Louder than Words 43
6. Evidence That Convicts 52
7. Shining Through the Storm 60
8. With Eyes Wide Open 68
9. God's Divine Appointment 75
10. Spiritual Warfare 84
11. Authentic Relationships 91
12. **When Things Don't Make Sense** 105
13. Hate: How We Hide, Deny, and Justify 110
14. Unleash the Power 118
15. Another Day ~ Another Decision 128
16. What's Hiding in Our Pockets? 134
17. The Effect Our Words Have 142
18. Brilliant Wisdom 152
19. Becoming Polished 159
20. Transforming Our Thoughts 167
21. The Spiritual Race 174
22. Compelled to a Life of Obedience 182
23. Confrontation: If, When, How 190
24. Activity Versus Busyness 198
25. Zapped by The Holy Spirit 209
26. Spiritual Nourishment 217
27. When We're Worried 226
28. Praise and Thanksgiving ~ Sacrifice and Joy 233
29. God Sees Our Brokenness 241
30. A Shining Legacy 249

∾ 1 ∾
We Are Who God Says We Are

*Our sense of worth is not a question of
giftedness, talent, intelligence, or beauty.
Your sense of personal worth comes
from knowing who you are as a child of God.*

~ Neil T. Anderson
Founder, Freedom in Christ Ministries

*Focus:
We shine
when we
understand
to Whom
we belong.*

SUSAN SHARES HER STORY:

I grew up in a home that accepted God's love, and I was expected to believe this same way. But I didn't feel loved by God.

After eight years of taking care of my friend, Holly, and her young son, Holly died of cancer. When Holly died, I felt alone. I knew mentally that I was loved by God, but I couldn't get my heart to agree. How could God let this happen? Didn't God care?

I pressed through the darkness, though, seeking to understand and searching for another sign of His love. After I was led to adopt Holly's young son, I finally understood God's great love for me when He adopted me into His family.

We know Jesus loves us . . . because the Bible tells us so. We have faith that God loves this huge world, but we may have difficulty believing He loves us individually when sickness invades our body, someone we love is taken away, we lose our job, can't pay our bills, or find it hard to get out of bed in the morning.
Or perhaps we struggle with God's love because we've judged ourselves. The shame and guilt of past offenses may have made us feel unworthy of love. Besides, how could God care about the

Notes

intimate details of a person's life? We feel like a tiny pinhead when compared to the universe.

The Bible reveals the character of God. Within the pages of His Word, we unwrap His love story like a gift. We learn that we're:

- Loved
- Cared for
- Adopted into God's Family
- Sealed and Set Apart

Let's examine these truths more closely, as if we're holding a magnifying glass. Imagine it's a scorching hot day. As we peer into the truth, may the reflecting sun start a fire that burns these truths into our hearts and minds.

Loved

Childhood memories and traumatic events can impact our self-worth and our view of God. Do any memories or events from your childhood contribute to how you view God and how you believe He sees you? Any current situation? What are they?

On a scale of one to ten, with ten being the greatest, how loved by God do you feel? Draw a heart around that number.

1   2   3   4   5   6   7   8   9   10

Maybe you feel God has withheld His love. Read the following Scriptures describing God's love. Personalize God's message by writing your name in the blank.

The LORD *appeared to him from afar, saying, "I have loved [_____], with an everlasting love; therefore, I have drawn you with lovingkindness.* Jeremiah 31:3

God so loved [_____], that He gave His only begotten Son, that [if _____] believes in Him shall not perish, but have eternal life. John 3:16

You formed my inward parts; You wove me [_____] in my mother's womb. I [_____] will give thanks to You, for I, [_____], am fearfully and wonderfully made; Wonderful are Your works, and my soul knows it very well. Psalm 139:13–14

The LORD your God is in your midst, a victorious warrior. He will exult over you, [_____] with joy, He will be quiet in His love, He will rejoice over you, [_____], with shouts of joy. Zephaniah 3:17

Romans 3:10 tells us we have all sinned. None of us are worthy to stand before a holy God. But because God loves us so much, He provided atonement for our sin. *Atonement* is defined as "a making up for an offense or injury; satisfaction; the reconciliation of God and humankind through the sacrificial death of Jesus Christ."[2]

Read 1 John 4:9–10. Who made atonement for us? Why was it necessary?

First Corinthians 6:20 tells us that we were bought with a price. The NLT says it's "a high price."

Read Romans 9:25. God tells us that He makes us His _____. And to the unloved, He makes them _____.

Being beloved by God is a life-changing epiphany.

In your opinion, are love and care synonyms? How are they the same? How are they different?

Let's explore this concept of love and care a bit further.

Notes

Cared for

God's affection gets more personal. He:

- Knows our names (**Isaiah 43:1**)
- Knows how many hairs we have on our heads (**Luke 12:7**)
- Tells us to call on Him (**Jeremiah 33:3**)
- Requests that we give Him our worries (**1 Peter 5:7**)
- Tells us how to live a very good life (**Proverbs 7:2**)

This list is only the beginning. Everything in the Bible points to God's deep care for each woman He has created. Ponder these synonyms for care: guard, handle, manage, heed, aid.

Read Psalm 139:17–18 and fill in the missing word:

How precious also are Your thoughts to me, O God! How vast is the sum of them! If I should count them, they would outnumber the _____ _____.

According to scientist Robert Krulwich, "If you assume a grain of sand has an average size, and you calculate how many grains are in a teaspoon and then multiply by all the beaches and deserts in the world, the Earth has roughly (and we're speaking very roughly here) 7.5×10^{18} grains of sand, or seven quintillion, five hundred quadrillion grains."[3]

I can't even write those numerals. The point is that it's unfathomable that God's thoughts outnumber the grains of sand. He never takes a break from thinking about us and all that concerns us.

Do you believe that God cares about you and that you are always on His mind? If yes, how does this understanding affect your mindset throughout your day? If no, what is the hardest part about believing?

Read Ephesians 2:10. What claim does God make about you?

Notes

Depending on your Bible translation, you may have answered *handiwork, masterpiece*, or *workmanship*. Write what workmanship means to you.

The Creator of the universe calls us a masterpiece — a finished product. The next time you are made to feel less-than, insignificant, or unworthy, recall that you're God's masterpiece.

There's more. Read Deuteronomy 32:10 and fill in the missing phrase: *He found him in a desert land, and in the howling waste of a wilderness; He encircled him, He cared for him, He guarded him as* _____ _____ .

When someone says to us, "You're the apple of my eye," we should be delighted. The phrase means the person cherishes us. The psalmist wrote: ***Keep me as the apple of the eye; hide me in the shadow of Your wings*** (Psalm 17:8).

The apple, or pupil, is considered the most delicate part of the eye. When we look into another person's eyes, we see our own reflection. Similarly, when God looks into our eyes, He sees His reflection. We're made in the image of Christ. Everything in creation shows how beautiful God is, and because we're made in His image, we're beautiful. We're precious, cherished, and beloved.

When God looks at you, what does He see?

Adopted into God's Family

In the story we opened with, Susan was able to grasp the significance of God's love after she adopted her son. Romans 8:15 tells us: ***You have received a spirit of adoption as sons by which we cry out, "Abba! Father!"***

Did you get that? We're in God's family! When we believe Jesus is the Son of God, that He died for our sins and rose again, and we trust Him as our Savior, we're adopted into God's family. We

Notes

weren't worthy on our own or accepted because of our good works. Being created in God's image is what gives us worth. God saw that we were worth dying for. We're His children.

Match the following verses to their reference. These describe your new identity:

___ Galatians 3:26   A. *Therefore you are no longer a slave, but a son; and if a son, then an heir through God.*

___ Galatians 4:7   B. *So then you are no longer strangers and aliens, but you are fellow citizens with the saints, and are of God's household.*

___ Ephesians 2:1   C. *I will be a father to you, and you shall be sons and daughters to Me," says the Lord Almighty.*

___ 2 Corinthians 6:18   D. *You are all sons of God through faith in Christ Jesus.*

The word "adoption" comes from the Latin word *adoptare* meaning "taken by choice."[4] God chose us to be part of His royal family.

What does adoption by God mean to you?

Read John 1:12. What right do we have when we receive Jesus Christ?

Our earthly fathers may be absent emotionally or physically, but our perfect heavenly Father never will be. He provides, protects, values, and cherishes. He models love, loyalty, forgiveness, and discipline. Although earthly fathers make mistakes, God never does.

As God's child, we have a new identity. This identity comes with privileges that include being sealed and set apart.

Sealed and Set Apart

In many cultures, a king's package or letter was stamped with a seal to show its authenticity. If the package lacked the seal, it was considered inauthentic. The royal seal on a package also indicated its great worth, because it belonged to the king. When we choose to put our faith in Jesus Christ, God sets his seal on us; we're sealed as children of God.

Read Ephesians 1:13. What happens after a person hears the truth and believes?

When a new believer is sealed by the Holy Spirit, she belongs to God; her eternal security is guaranteed. God is the King of kings, and she is authentically His.

Now that makes for a beautiful package.

In what way will believing that you're stamped with God's seal of approval change how you react when others disapprove of you?

Now read Psalm 4:3 and fill in the missing word:

Know that the Lord has _____ the godly man for Himself; the Lord hears when I call to Him.

By bearing God's seal, we're also set apart to obey His commandments. What follows are His blessings. To be set apart is to be saved or used for a particular purpose. In this way, we're set apart to shine His love and point others to Him. This means we'll be different — not following after what this world loves.

The NLT paraphrases Philippians 2:15 this way:

Live clean, innocent lives as children of God, shining like bright lights in a world full of crooked and perverse people.

How are you set apart and shining like a bright light in your workplace, home, and community?

Notes

Let's revisit our personal assessment: On a scale of one to ten, with ten being the greatest, how loved by God do you feel now? Draw a heart around that number.

1   2   3   4   5   6   7   8   9   10

Our actions reflect what we believe about God, our identity in Him, His purpose for us, and our mission is on earth. With these truths burned into our heart, we'll confidently light up any room.

What Meant the Most to You from Today's Study?

Application

- On colorful sticky notes rewrite the verses containing your name. Put these on your mirrors, refrigerator, car dashboard, or any place they can be a constant reminder of God's love for you. Share them with your daughters, granddaughters, or any other women you love.

- Make a sand bag as a reminder that God is thinking about you. Purchase blue paper, a small, clear, plastic jewelry bag (3 inches by 2 inches) at a craft store and a bag of children's play sand. Scoop a bit of sand into one bag and seal the bag. Write on a piece of blue paper, "God Constantly Thinks About Me" (Psalm 139:17–18). Staple the note to the bag of sand. Keep it on the vanity or nightstand as a visual reminder of God's love. Make extra sets to share with others.

- Create a "Love Myself Alphabet." On a lined piece of paper, write the letters of the alphabet, one on each line. Next to each letter write a word that describes you. For example, A= adopted by God, B= beautiful, C= cared for, etc.

- Listen to "Who You Say I Am," by Hillsong. https://www.youtube.com/watch?v=lKw6uqtGFfo

Light from the Scriptures

No man will be able to stand before you all the days of your life. Just as I have been with Moses, I will be with you; I will not fail you or forsake you. Be strong and courageous, for you shall give this people possession of the land which I swore to their fathers to give them. Only be strong and very courageous; be careful to do according to all the law which Moses My servant commanded you; do not turn from it to the right or to the left, so that you may have success wherever you go. This book of the law shall not depart from your mouth, but you shall meditate on it day and night, so that you may be careful to do according to all that is written in it; for then you will make your way prosperous, and then you will have success. Have I not commanded you? Be strong and courageous! Do not tremble or be dismayed, for the Lord your God is with you wherever you go.

Joshua 1:5–9

Notes

Our actions reflect what we believe about God, our identity in Him, His purpose for us, and our mission on earth. With these truths burned into our heart, we'll confidently light up any room.

Notes

*Focus:
We shine
when we listen
to God.*

༄ 2 ༄
Listening to God

*One can approach the Bible with a cold, rationalistic attitude,
or one can do so with reverence and the desire to hear God speak.*

~ Billy Graham

> WHILE AT MY SEVEN-YEAR-OLD SON'S BASEBALL GAME, I LEARNED an important principle:
>
> The game was tied and the bases were loaded. Will's team got up to bat. As soon as Will's teammate hit the ball, every coach from both sides began yelling orders:
>
> "Run here!'
>
> "Throw the ball to first!"
>
> "Run to third!"
>
> "Go home!"
>
> All the parents were cheering, and clapping, and shouting. The game was organized confusion and mayhem.
>
> I wondered, *How do all these boys know what to do with everyone screaming directions? They surely must be trained to recognize and focus only on their coach's voice.*
>
> Then God whispered to my heart. *You, too, have many voices influencing you. Train your ears to identify mine.*
>
> God used a boys' ballgame to demonstrate a life-changing principle. Fifteen years later, I still ask God to help me recognize His voice.

Have you ever thought or wished God would tell you what to do, then you'd do it? Maybe you're wondering if God really speaks at all — at least to you. Do you think God speaks to others more than you? If so, whom does He talk with more?

When God does speak to you, what method does He use?

When are you most likely to hear Him?

If you're not hearing God speak, what do you think is blocking His voice?

Maybe you feel uncomfortable with the way in which you responded to those questions. Complete honesty can provoke that emotion. Most of us desire to know what God thinks is best regarding our personal lives and would also agree that we experience seasons when God appears to be silent.

Our lives can be busy — full of distractions, many of which are good. With so much information bombarding us at once, discerning the right voice can be difficult, even confusing.

On any given day, what voices are you tuned into? Include social media, television, work, friends, and family.

Read John 10:3–4. Who is the Good Shepherd?

How does He identify the sheep who belong to Him?

Notes

How is the Good Shepherd like a coach?

Why do the sheep follow Him?

Jesus clearly articulates that His people follow Him because they hear — His whisper, His nudging, His impression.

First Kings 17 describes a wild time when Elijah was literally running for his life. He had killed the false prophets and now Jezebel wanted to murder him. Elijah was disheartened. The "voices in his head" had instigated a great big pity party. Eventually, he safely reached a cave in Mt. Horeb. While quiet in a cave, Elijah heard from God.

Read 1 Kings 19:11–12. How is God's voice described? Circle all that apply.

a gentle blowing	a whisper	an earthquake
a fierce wind	a still, small voice	a fire

The noise we create or surround ourselves with may drown out the gentle voice of God. Even the good work we do for God — serving and teaching, for example — can become a confusing time when we're surrounded by the world's influence. Our culture's persuasion can hinder our ability to hear God's voice. We must be intentional and tune out the lies being shouted at us so we can distinguish His still, small voice. How would you define *noise*?

Noise can be both a noun and a verb. As a noun, noise is defined as "loud, confused, or senseless shouting or outcry." As a verb, noise is defined as "to talk much or loudly . . . or spread by rumor."[5]

Our brain must sort through and process hundreds of pieces of information daily. All information is either true or false. God is all truth. Anything contrary to the truth is a lie.

Read John 8:44. How is the devil identified?

Read John 10:10. What three things does the thief — the devil — come to do?

The devil delivers a message contrary to God's truth. He uses social media, secular magazines, and television to bombard us with lies in an attempt to *kill* our self-worth and value. An innocent trip to the grocery store leaves us feeling worthless or inferior when we're forced to wade through the sea of magazines near the registers. You know the ones — the magazines suggesting we should look a certain way or be a specific size. They imply we are not pretty enough, thin enough, smart enough, or gifted enough. The devil fights to *steal* our joy. He tries to conceal the truth. His desire is to use twisted perversion to *destroy* any right thinking.

The following lies are some of the devil's most popular noisemakers:

- You're not beautiful.
- Everyone is doing it, so should you.
- Adultery isn't the worst sin.
- You deserve that, even if you go in debt to get it.
- Get to the top at all costs.
- You deserve to know what she said.
- Worrying about them means you love them more.
- You're not as gifted or talented as other people.
- Your shameful past disqualifies you from being used by God.
- You messed up . . . again.

Notes

Which lie, either from the list above, or one you're currently dealing with, is easiest for you to believe?

Another lie the devil shouts is that a compromise of our values will bring ultimate satisfaction. He shouts we will find the answer to fulfillment and happiness in self, success, and good times. Why do you think it's so easy to accept lies as truth?

We live in a sin-infiltrated world. But here's good news. John 16:13 tells us this: *When He, the Spirit of truth, comes, He will guide you into all the truth; for He will not speak on His own initiative, but whatever He hears, He will speak; and He will disclose to you what is to come.*

Using the previous verse, underline what the Holy Spirit — the Spirit of truth — guides us in. The Holy Spirit exposes deceit and wrong motives; He opens our eyes to the truth. He helps us hear God's voice.

In Psalm 119:18 we read: *Open my eyes, that I may behold wonderful things from Your law.* How is opening our spiritual eyes to see the same as opening our ears to hear?

Dr. Charles Stanley, founder of InTouch Ministries, writes

> The Bible is our guidebook to God's thoughts and actions. It is the primary source for Christians to discover His character and learn to trust Him. This means we ought to read more than just a little bit every day. Our goal should be to absorb the message and then listen for God to offer instructions on how and where to apply His Word."[6]

God spoke to the people in the Bible, and He's speaking to us today.

- Sometimes He uses another person to help us discern His truth. Seek out godly friends who keep you accountable and pray for you.

- Often God will gently whisper to our hearts and remind us of something we've read in the Bible or of a biblical principle, the way He did for me at the ballgame. But to recall what's in the Bible means we must be familiar with what's in it.

- The Bible is His main way of talking to us. The historical accounts teach us what to do and what not to do. Jesus' stories teach us how to live. It's imperative we spend time each day in quiet, focused Bible reading. We can use a journal to write down what we read. We can make it personal by substituting our name into the message.

- Finally, we can say to God we're waiting expectantly for Him to speak.

Often, we must wait for God's answer to a specific prayer. During this pause, however, God still speaks. With the rising of the morning sun, He reminds us He's faithful — He hasn't forgotten about us, our prayers, or our needs. With each predictable low and high tide, the ocean speaks that God is still in control. While we listen to the bird sing, God tells us He'll take care of us too. And the mountains provide a majestic visual of God's strength — our mighty fortress and strong tower — our Rock.

Matthew 13:43 tells us *the righteous will shine like the sun in the kingdom of their Father. Whoever has ears, let them hear* (NIV).

Whose voice are you listening to today?

What Meant the Most to You from Today's Study?

Notes

> Our culture's persuasion can deafen our ability to hear God's voice. We must be intentional and tune out the lies being shouted at us so we can distinguish His still, small voice.

Application

- Purchase a journal to use during your Bible-reading time. Each day write the date at the top. Write down the chapter and verses you're reading. If you're reading from a devotion book, get your Bible and read the verses the devotional references. Seeing it for yourself makes a difference. Summarize what you read. Then, write down how the passage or verses apply to you.

- Make yourself a "cave," "prayer closet," or "war room" — a special place where you meet with God. Your place can be a special corner of your kitchen, a chair in the living room, a rocker on the front porch, or a walk-in closet.

- Read Chip Ingram's book *Good to Great in God's Eyes*.

- Listen to "Word of God Speak" by MercyMe. https://www.youtube.com/watch?v=4JK_6osCH74

Light from the Scriptures

See, I have set before you today life and prosperity, and death and adversity; in that I command you today to love the LORD your God, to walk in His ways and to keep His commandments and His statutes and His judgments, that you may live and multiply, and that the LORD your God may bless you in the land where you are entering to possess it. But if your heart turns away and you will not obey, but are drawn away and worship other gods and serve them, I declare to you today that you shall surely perish. You will not prolong your days in the land where you are crossing the Jordan to enter and possess it. I call heaven and earth to witness against you today, that I have set before you life and death, the blessing and the curse. So choose life in order that you may live, you and your descendants, by loving the LORD your God, by obeying His voice, and by holding fast to Him; for this is your life and the length of your days, that you may live in the land which the LORD swore to your fathers, to Abraham, Isaac, and Jacob, to give them.

Deuteronomy 30:15–20

❧ 3 ❧
Darkened with Disappointment

If the truth were known, the saints of God in every age were only effective after they had been wounded.

~ A. W. Tozer
Author and Pastor

> **Notes**
>
> *Focus: We shine when hope eclipses disappointment.*

I EARNESTLY PRAYED FOR A PERSON I LOVED TO FIND EMPLOYMENT. For weeks I made this my top priority. Then one day, the good news came — this person had found a job. My joy shone on my face — I literally couldn't stop smiling. I cranked up the volume on the Christian radio station, and I sang along to the praise music. I thanked God for answered prayer.

But the next day, I learned there was a mistake and my friend didn't have the job after all.

Initially, shock and confusion occupied my thoughts. But soon those feelings were surpassed with anger . . . *toward God*. Without hesitation, I ranted, "Wouldn't it have been better to not have answered my prayer at all than to seemingly answer it, and then snatch it back?"

I was unable to articulate my thoughts further. Disappointment left me feeling dark, like a candle had been blown out.

Disappointment is defined as "unhappiness from the failure of something hoped for or expected to happen; someone or something that fails to satisfy hopes or expectations."[7] Dictionary.com goes further to say "the feeling of sadness or displeasure caused by the nonfulfillment of one's hopes or expectations."[8] Synonyms include *dismay, dissatisfaction, frustration, let down, disillusionment, sadness, regret.*

Notes

We've all experienced disappointment, either as a passing emotion or the result of a more permanent situation. When dreams aren't realized, expectations aren't met, or desires are left unfulfilled, sadness and disappointment result.

Sometimes it's people who disappoint us.
- Your child makes poor choices.
- Your marriage isn't what you hoped it would be.
- You wrote your best paper, but your professor disagrees.
- Someone you love lets you down.
- You prayed about something very important and sought godly counsel, but things still didn't work out the way you had imagined.

At other times, situations bring disappointment.
- You didn't get the raise or promotion you thought you deserved.
- An illness attacked your body as soon as you retired from your job.
- You received the news that you wouldn't be able to have a baby.

Has there been a time you were paralyzed with disappointment and didn't know how to pick up the broken pieces? Describe those feelings.

Has there been a time you felt like you were a disappointment? What made you feel that way?

If you're being completely transparent, has there been a time — even momentarily — when you felt that God let you down?

Do you think we can disappoint God? If so, in what ways? If not, why?

Notes

Does God have an expectation of us?

The Bible tells us God has emotions. For example, God gets angry. He loves. He has mercy. We sin against God. But to disappoint Him means He would have to have an expectation of us. God remembers we are made from dust. He tells us in Romans 3:10: *There is no one righteous, not even one* (NASB). God doesn't expect perfection. We might disobey Him, but we're not a disappointment to Him.

The Bible is full of people who experienced disappointment: Moses, Sarah, Job, Jacob, Hannah, and Rachel, to name some. The disciples believed Jesus was the Savior, and then they saw Him crucified and buried.

Read John 11:1–45. Mary, Martha, and Lazarus were siblings and close friends with Jesus. When Lazarus became sick, the sisters sent a message to Jesus. What did the message say? (John 11:3)

What do you think they expected Jesus to do?

But Jesus didn't come for two more days and by that time Lazarus had died. How do you think the sisters felt at that point?

Notes

When Martha finally saw Jesus, she said something very significant. What was it? (John 11:21)

What do you think Martha was *really* saying?

"If you had been here" reveals an attitude of belief in Jesus and His capabilities. But it also indicates a shift in emotions: blame and an unmet expectation. Martha expected Jesus to come, and because He didn't, Lazarus died. She couldn't see past her disappointment to understand that Jesus had a purpose in His delay.

How did Jesus respond?

How did the miracle affect the people watching? (John 11:45)

Martha blamed Jesus for poor timing that led to Lazarus' death. I blamed God for my disappointment when the job for my friend didn't work out. Neither of our expectations were met, and we both were left feeling disappointed. Later, Martha saw the greater miracle — that many believed. My friend eventually found a better job. I may never understand why God had the situation play out like it did, but that's not my place to know. God had a purpose in it, and that has to be enough.

Looking back at your own disappointment, are you able to see the greater purpose, as in Martha's case? If so, describe it.

Disappointments are part of life. But if disappointment isn't dealt with, it can grow into depression and despair. Despair can then blossom into full-blown doubt, causing us to question our faith.

I found hope in the following suggestions. They provide ways to help us deal with disappointment quickly and honestly.

1. Pray.

Now isn't the time to blame God and run away from Him. Run *to* Him. Be completely real and transparent with God. Cry and rant and tell Him how you really feel. Talk with Him like you would your best friend. He already knows what you're thinking anyway, so you have nothing to hide.

Read Philippians 4:6–7. What can we pray about?

Does this include disappointments? Why or why not?

Accept that it's okay to not see the whole picture as God does. Begin to operate from a place of trust. Martha and I both had limited vision. But because her story is recorded, we have the opportunity to see the bigger picture and the end result.

Read Romans 8:28. Bad things happen. Yet God can make something good come from our disappointments.

What is the condition attached to the above verse?

Are you willing to trust the One you love?

Notes

2. Be thankful.

Acknowledge what God has done for you. Express gratitude for the specific gifts and blessings — past and present — He has given to you and others. Instead of allowing disappointment to weigh us down, we can tip the balance scale by being thankful for the other ways God has worked in our life.

What are you thankful for?

3. Praise.

Praise is complimenting God for His virtues, attributes, and excellence. As we gain insight into God's character, we admire Him and His perfection. Praise shifts the focus from ourselves and our situations, and places the focus on God.

Which of God's attributes can you praise Him for today?

4. Adjust your expectations.

Read Psalm 73:23–26: *Nevertheless, I am continually with You; You have taken hold of my right hand. With Your counsel You will guide me, and afterward receive me to glory. Whom have I in heaven but You? And besides You, I desire nothing on earth. My flesh and my heart may fail, but God is the strength of my heart and my portion forever.*

People will fail us, and we'll disappoint others. According to this passage, what does God say He'll do?

Read Romans 15:13. How is God described? What does He provide?

Romans 5:5 tells us *hope does not disappoint, because the love of God has been poured out within our hearts through the Holy Spirit who was given to us.*

God is our hope and He loves us so much!

5. Get moving.

Stop thinking about your disappointment. Concentrate on a new hobby. Read inspirational books. Start a prayer group or Bible study. What is something you would like to try? What are you interested in?

6. Rethink your plans, ideas, and motives.

God is working in the lives of the people who disappoint us. He is also transforming how we respond to disappointment — even disappointment with God. Set aside time to evaluate what God is teaching you.

What have you discovered about God that you hadn't realized before?

What have you learned about yourself?

7. Refresh yourself by reading God's Word.

Meditating on God's Word always brings strength and encouragement. Deuteronomy 31:6 tells us: *Be strong and courageous, do not be afraid or tremble at them, for the Lord your God is the one who goes with you. He will not fail you or forsake you.*

We're never alone — especially in our disappointments. When will you schedule time to meet with God to tell Him about your disappointments?

Notes

8. **Expect to be revived.**

Read Isaiah 57:15 and fill in the missing words: *God will* _____ *the* _____.

Our disappointment won't last forever. Visualize your good future. What does it look like?

God will use our disappointments to mold us into the person He wants us to be. And He will use the situations for His glory — to point us and others to Him. Hold on to this hope found in Job 11:17: *Your life would be brighter than noonday; Darkness would be like the morning.*

What Meant the Most to You from Today's Study?

Application

➢ Habakkuk 3:17–18 tells us this: *Though the fig tree should not blossom and there be no fruit on the vines, though the yield of the olive should fail and the fields produce no food, though the flock should be cut off from the fold and there be no cattle in the stalls, yet I will exult in the Lord, I will rejoice in the God of my salvation.*

Rewrite these verses with your special circumstance:

Though _____,

though _____,

though _____,

I will _____.

➢ Read: Priscilla Shirer's book *God Is Able*.

➢ Listen to "Living Hope," by Phil Wickham.
https://www.youtube.com/watch?v=u-1fwZtKJSM

Light from the Scriptures

Yours, O Lord, is the greatness and the power and the glory and the victory and the majesty, indeed everything that is in the heavens and the earth; Yours is the dominion, O Lord, and You exalt Yourself as head over all. Both riches and honor come from You, and You rule over all, and in Your hand is power and might; and it lies in Your hand to make great and to strengthen everyone. Now therefore, our God, we thank You, and praise Your glorious name.

1 Chronicles 29:11–13

Notes

)(We're never alone — especially in our disappointment.)(

Notes

*Focus:
We shine
when
we love others.*

❧ 4 ❧
Loving People in a Diverse Culture

In the New Testament, love is more of a verb than a noun. It has more to do with acting than a feeling. The call to love is not so much a call to a certain state of feeling as it is to a quality of action.

~ R. C. Sproul
Author and Pastor

At a festival, I witnessed these events:

Standing on a riser, a man used a bullhorn to yell at the people as they walked by.

"You're going to hell," he announced. "Repent from your sins."

As he scolded and judged, he never made eye contact. My body language revealed disgust at the man's approach. My son, Will, grabbed my arm and pleaded, "Mom, don't say anything." I didn't. The man continued his reprimanding rant.

A minute later, I overheard a lady say, "If you're gonna call yourself a Christian, you should act like one."

Will and I continued walking down the street and noticed a gathering of fifty or more people. An organization had attracted a crowd to its peaceful atmosphere. I observed several men and women handing out bottled water and engaging in personal conversations. People sat and relaxed to the sound of calming music, while the organizers passed out information about their New-Age, Jesus-less congregation.

We live in a culturally diverse country. (*Diverse* means showing a great deal of variety; differing from one another.) If everyone held the same standards and beliefs, then loving others would be easy. Or at least easier. But we don't.

Politics, social preferences, and religious organizations are often the bricks we use to build divisive walls. As Christ-followers, we are called to demolish walls and establish relationships so we can point others to Jesus and what He did on the cross.

Recall Matthew 5:16: *Let your light shine before men in such a way that they may see your good works, and glorify your Father who is in heaven.*

Our light can shine because of an outpouring of God's love and grace. We're compelled to shine this light because of God's love. Because He lives in us, we radiate His light.

Reflect on the story at the beginning of this chapter. Concerning the lady who said, "You should act like a Christian"— what do you suppose she thought a Christian should act like?

The man shouting commands through the bullhorn spoke truth. We do need to repent of our sins. How would you describe the manner in which he delivered his message?

Why do you think the water-giving organization drew such a large crowd?

Jesus drew large crowds. Read John 6:5–10. Noting the large crowd that followed Him, Jesus asked Phillip a question. What was the question?

What did Jesus direct the crowd to do? (v. 10)

Notes

What do you discover about Jesus' approach?

If we follow Jesus' example, how are we to approach people who don't know God's love?

Jesus approached people compassionately. Read John 8:3–11. What can you deduce about Jesus's posture and eye contact?

The scribes and Pharisees came forward with an adulterous woman and said the law of Moses commanded she be stoned. How did Jesus respond? (v. 10)

Jesus had another encounter with an adulterous woman. This time He went against cultural taboos when He spoke to her. Samaritans and Jews avoided each other, so it was already an eyebrow-lifting situation just to be a Jew passing through Samaria. It was here that Jesus met the person we call The Woman at the Well.

Read John 4:7–15. How did Jesus interact with the Samarian woman?

How did He respond to her sin?

Jesus felt compassion and love for those He interacted with. He didn't, however, water down the truth or excuse sinful behavior. He didn't justify or make exceptions.

Back to the man with the bullhorn. We don't know if he was being obedient and boldly proclaiming the truth. But what the listeners heard didn't compel them to stay. His message was not heard because it wasn't spoken in love. His screaming rant, in fact, could be mistaken for hate.

If we want to shine for Jesus, we must love people.

Read John 21:15–17. What question did Jesus ask Simon Peter, son of John, three times?

Each time, Jesus gave the same direction:

_____ My lambs. (v. 15)

_____ My sheep. (v. 16)

_____ My sheep. (v. 17)

Depending on your translation, you may have read the following words:

Feed   take care of   tend   shepherd

other_____

These synonyms indicate action. How can we show we care?

Read Mark 16:15. What did Jesus tell His disciples before His ascension into heaven?

Notes

Go — a verb, commanding we feed His sheep with the message of the gospel. Where is your current mission field? Who are your sheep?

We share the gospel to those we come in contact with — within our sphere of influence.

Back to the initial question, but from a different perspective. How do you think a Christian ought to act?

Reflect. *What's your personal story? When did God show up in your life at just the right time? What has God saved you from?* Your answers to these questions, and other questions like them, are what compel others to stay and listen. Others can argue about "religion," but they can't argue with the reality of your story. This is how you love like Jesus. This is how you feed the hungry and give hope to those who are thirsty for a miracle in their lives. When they see what Jesus has done in your life, they want Jesus in their lives too.

Read Colossians 3:12–13 written here:

As those who have been chosen of God, holy and beloved, put on a heart of compassion, kindness, humility, gentleness and patience; bearing with one another, and forgiving each other, whoever has a complaint against anyone; just as the Lord forgave you, so also should you. Beyond all these things put on love, which is the perfect bond of unity.

Circle the words that identify what we need to "put on."

Shining the light in a dark community begins with loving people — because we know Jesus loves them, and it's through His eyes we see them. We don't have to be perfect or have our lives together for the light to shine or for God's love to spill out. We only have to be willing for God to fill us with His love for people so we can respond in ways that draw others to Him. We aren't accountable to everyone throughout the world, but we are liable for those people we come in contact with. Even people who choose to live in darkness see the light when they interact with us (Matthew 4:16).

Let's ask ourselves: *Would others want to be a Christian based on what they see in me? Do others want my God? Am I pointing others to Christ or turning them away with a hateful or judgmental attitude?* If you're unsure how to answer these questions, ask God to help you respond in the way He wants. In the next chapter, you'll find practical ways to show love to other people. Perhaps you're doing many of the suggested actions already. Maybe you'll try something new.

Jesus is love. That is the message of the gospel. When others observe God's love shining in us, they will want Jesus too.

What Meant the Most to You from Today's Study?

Application

> The next chapter, "Actions Speak Louder Than Words," is dedicated to sharing practical ways to love others. Take time to ask God to prepare your heart and provide you with the passion and inspiration to do what He wants you to do.

> Listen to "Go Light Your World" by Kathy Troccoli. https://www.youtube.com/watch?v=CVqR6kTu8lE

Notes

Light from the Scriptures

How blessed is he whose transgression is forgiven, whose sin is covered! How blessed is the man to whom the LORD does not impute iniquity, and in whose spirit there is no deceit! When I kept silent about my sin, my body wasted away through my groaning all day long. For day and night Your hand was heavy upon me; my vitality was drained away as with the fever heat of summer. Selah. I acknowledged my sin to You, and my iniquity I did not hide; I said, "I will confess my transgressions to the LORD"; and You forgave the guilt of my sin. Selah. Therefore, let everyone who is godly pray to You in a time when You may be found; surely in a flood of great waters they will not reach him. You are my hiding place; You preserve me from trouble;

You surround me with songs of deliverance. Selah. I will instruct you and teach you in the way which you should go; I will counsel you with My eye upon you.

Psalm 32:1–8

> We only have to be willing for God to fill us with His love for people so we can respond in ways that draw others to Him.

❦ 5 ❦
Actions Speak Louder Than Words

*We are told to let our light shine, and if it does,
we won't need to tell anybody it does.
Lighthouses don't fire cannons to call attention to their shining
— they just shine.*

~ Dwight L. Moody
Evangelist

Focus: We shine brightly in a dark, diverse culture.

I MET JOYCE AT A CHRISTMAS GATHERING. ALTHOUGH WE didn't know each other personally, we had both heard about each other. I was told she was gay and that her daughter had cancer; she was told I teach a Bible study class.

I approached Joyce and asked about her daughter. She was eager to talk and told me she would be traveling across the country to be with her daughter within the next few days.

When Joyce returned from her visit, I emailed her and inquired about her daughter's condition. She filled me in but then said something that really pained me.

"You're the only person outside my small group to ask about my daughter. The 'church' people egged my house when they heard I was living there."

"We have obvious differences," I responded, "but we're also alike — we're both mothers who love our daughters."

It saddened me to think this mother was going through her daughter's cancer without much support. I wouldn't want anyone to go through that.

Joyce and I became friends. She accepted me and I was able to share with her about the love of Christ. Three years later, she continues to ask me to pray.

Relationships don't always start like this or end up like this either. Our common love for our daughters enabled me to show Joyce God's love for both of them.

The following are practical ways in which we can shine in a dark, diverse society. Not every suggestion will be at every person's comfort level. But by becoming aware of the people around us, we're given the opportunity to make an impact for the kingdom of God.

Smile

A smile is non-verbal communication.[10] It transmits warmth, friendship, and concern. It has a positive effect on others. (This is not referring to an unnatural smile plastered on our face.) When we make eye contact and genuinely smile, either widely, or a closed-lip grin, we show acceptance.

Smile at your co-worker, someone new to Bible study, or the cashier at the grocery store. A smile could be the start of a conversation. A recent survey revealed that a smile or a nod helps people feel more connected to others. But when people are ignored by a stranger or get the cold shoulder, they feel disconnected.[11] At some point, others may want to know the source of your smile.

When were you impacted by a smile or lack of a smile?

What keeps you from smiling?

What other ways can you acknowledge a person?

Resist the urge to be offended when someone doesn't smile back or acknowledge you. They may have many burdens that distract them.

Ask About a Person's Tattoo

More than twenty years ago, I was registering a new student for college courses. "Tell me about your tattoo," I said. Hearing her story, I learned more about her as a person and discovered my question, although simple, was a powerful way to break down barriers.

People are usually glad to share their story, and we may find that we have something in common. Commonalities generate connection. I liken tattoos on a body to charm bracelets dangling around the wrist. Charms represent what a person loves. In a similar way, tattoos are charms that are permanently engraved on the body. Both charms and tattoos present an opportunity for building a bridge for communication and an opportunity to share your testimony.

What other ways can you make connections?

Encourage

Encouragement can be verbal or written. Sometimes a few words of encouragement make a person's day better. Make or buy a card for someone you know needs to be lifted up. You could include "Some Things I Like about You" in the card. (This is especially effective with children and teens.) Leave the card in a conspicuous place, or send it through the mail. Email, texts, and Facebook notes are effective, but tangible notes and cards can be displayed and kept forever. For others, a phone call can make their day.

Hebrews 10:25 reminds us to encourage one another. Who can you encourage today?

Bake a Cake . . . Fix a Meal

Most of us can deliver food to people, even if cooking is not our "cup of tea." Grocery stores, restaurants, and catering services make it easy to purchase delicious meals.

Notes

Notes

When I was in a particularly challenging season, my friend Beverly said, "Your cup is running over, so I figured your plate should be too," as she set baskets of fruit, hot chili, homemade cookies, and baked spaghetti on my kitchen table. Beverly is the kind of woman I think of when I read about Dorcas in the Bible.

Dorcas is only mentioned once in the Bible — in Acts 9:36. Read this verse. What made Dorcas a stand-out gal? How did she spend her time?

What are other ways you can serve people that don't involve food?

Be Generous

Once a young woman told me about her desperate financial situation. After God's leading, I left a card and a little money on her desk but never said anything to her. Several hours later, she tearfully walked into my office. She exclaimed, "God is so good!" She understood the gift was from God.

In what ways do you consider yourself to be a generous person, with money or with your time?

Do you ever feel it's difficult to be generous to others when you're in need yourself? How so?

Proverbs 11:25 provides hope. What does it say about a person who refreshes another?

Notes

When, if ever, did you refresh someone and feel refreshed yourself?

Being generous with our time can include such things as babysitting for a single mom who needs to do an errand, helping a friend with a project, or driving someone to the doctor. God doesn't expect us to do everything. But we can all do something.

How has God been generous to you?

Include Someone Not Normally in Your Group

Have you ever been at work or church with people you see regularly and heard them making lunch plans — but not with you? Ouch. We may feel left out, regardless of whether or not we wanted to go.

Has that ever happened to you? If so, how did you feel?

Is there a similar situation where you felt left out?

Have you ever been on the other side of that situation and been among the women planning lunch and inadvertently didn't notice someone close by — until you returned?

Inviting someone into the group is a kind, thoughtful gesture. Being ostracized can lead to loneliness and affect our self-worth. Inviting another to join you puts the decision of acceptance on the other person. But at least, you've extended the welcome.

Author and theologian, J. D. Greear writes, "As You have been to me (God), so I will be to others."[11] How has God been to you? What has He done?

Based on how you described God's work in your life, how will you respond to others?

Listen

In a 2012 article titled "Look 'Em in the Eye," authors Brett and Kate McKay wrote, "Sociologists tell us that people are starved for attention. Despite the fact that we're more 'connected' than ever, folks are hungry for face-to-face interactions and someone [who will] really, sincerely listen to them."

Are you surprised by that statement? Why or why not?

Once when I was checking out at the grocery store, I looked the clerk (who normally frowned and was generally unpleasant) in the eye and asked her how she was. "My mother is in the hospital," the older woman responded. I promised to pray and told her I would check in with her over the next few days. From that moment on, the woman always asked me to come through her line.

Why do you think the clerk suddenly encouraged me to come through her checkout?

Eye contact shows others they have our attention. Listening well and making eye contact may mean we have to slow down to make intentional contact. If we're always in a hurry, we'll be too distracted to listen.

James 1:19 tells us to be quick to _____.

Think about a time when someone took extra time to listen to you. How did it make you feel?

Call People by Name

Sometimes remembering a person's name is hard. But names are important. Calling a person by name shows we value them. God knows all of our names. Read Isaiah 43:1 and fill your name in the blank. Then describe how this personal message affects you.

I have called you by name, _____;
you are Mine.

This verse is personal and powerful. How do these words make you feel?

Do you find it difficult to remember names? If you do, what are ways you can remember them?

Avoid Drama, Gossip, and Unhealthy Conflict

Simply walk away from it. We will feel uplifted, have a better attitude, and be more inspired to pursue worthy things when we're not entertaining this type of negative activity.

Where do you encounter drama, gossip, and conflict?

Notes

Practically speaking, what can you do to avoid it?

Read 1 Thessalonians 4:11. How would you summarize this verse?

A quiet life doesn't imply a life without words, but rather one without chaos. And "minding our own business" is definitely part of a peaceful existence.

These suggestions may seem minor but when practiced, they make a major impact. With our words and actions, we demonstrate God's love, and people are drawn to Him. Isn't that what it's all about? Go ahead . . . shine bright!

What Meant the Most to You from Today's Study?

Application

> This chapter offered practical ways we can shine the light and radiate the love of Jesus. The ideas may appear simple, but the response they evoke can be life changing. Not all of these suggestions will work for you. Find those that do work, and allow God to help you make a difference in another person's life.

> Listen to "Shine on" by NeedToBreathe: https://www.youtube.com/watch?v=zqPGbGUlcjY

Light from the Scriptures

Seven times a day I praise You, because of Your righteous ordinances. Those who love Your law have great peace, and nothing causes them to stumble. I hope for Your salvation, O Lord, and do Your commandments. My soul keeps Your testimonies, and I love them exceedingly.

Psalm 119:164–167

Notes

⋇
A quiet life doesn't imply one without words, but rather one without chaos. And "minding our own business" is definitely part of a peaceful existence.
⋇

~ 6 ~
Evidence That Convicts

Fruit of the Spirit working through millions of believers by faith could literally change the world.

–Dr. Bill Bright
Founder and President, Campus Crusade for Christ International

Focus: We shine when there's evidence of new life in Jesus Christ.

> Covered in a mixture of chocolate ice cream and dirt, five-year-old Will came running into the house screaming with excitement.
>
> "Mom, Dad, I found a bird egg!" he proudly declared. "It's white with bluish-gray speckles."
>
> After chatting about God's creation, my husband and I explained the egg needed to go back in the nest so its mother could take care of it. Will left to return the egg to its nest.
>
> Within moments, however, he came back into the kitchen. "Mom, I didn't get to put the egg back." His mouth hung open in surprise. "I don't know what happened. I put the egg in my pocket and then . . . something strange happened . . . and there's a baby bird!" he finally said.
>
> Will and his dad settled the baby bird back into its nest right away. Later that night I found Will's pants on the washing machine. I pulled the pocket inside out and there it was — evidence that new life had begun. Fragments of eggshells and blood filled the pocket lining.
>
> Alone in the dimly lit laundry room, I stood silent.
>
> If I hadn't seen the evidence, I wouldn't have believed it. New life actually began in my son's pants pocket.
>
> My heart felt a gentle impression that asked, *What about you? Is there evidence God has put new life in you?*

It's a loaded question, but one necessary for us to ask ourselves: Is there evidence I'm a Christ-follower? Maybe it's a difficult question to answer now. Let's study God's Word, discern what evidence of new life looks like, and come back to this question in a bit.

For starters, let's talk about "evidence."

Evidence is defined as "an outward sign."[13]

All kinds of people make up society. What appears to be most evident in our society are the numerous philosophies — many of which accept sinful behavior — and shifting moral beliefs. This may contribute to the confusion associated with evidences of Christ-like behavior.

In Pew Research Center telephone surveys conducted in 2018 and 2019, 65% of American adults describe themselves as Christians when asked about their religion, down 12 percentage points over the past decade. Meanwhile, the religiously unaffiliated share of the population, consisting of people who describe their religious identity as atheist, agnostic or "nothing in particular," now stands at 26%, up from 17% in 2009.[14]

Does this statistic surprise you? Why or why not?

In what ways does our culture reflect 65% of its population following Christ? What evidence, for and against, makes this statistic debatable?

Do you think some people label themselves as Christians because they don't fit into the "other" group?

How do you define Christianity? Is it a noun (name) only or a verb (action)? How so?

Notes

Notes

How is Christianity different from other religions?

Paul, the writer of Galatians, wrote about his past behavior and the evidence of his new life. Read Galatians 1:13. What did Paul — first called Saul — do to any person who followed Jesus?

But then, while traveling a dusty road, Saul was blinded by God's light. He believed Jesus was Lord and Savior and his life was forever changed — starting with a new name.

Paul made clear that a conversion on the inside, reveals a visible transformation on the outside — evidence of a changed life.

Evidence of new life in Jesus Christ is called *fruit*. Read Galatians 5:22–23. List the fruit named in these verses.

_____   _____

_____   _____

_____   _____

_____   _____

_____

You may be overwhelmed by such an ambitious list. Or, out of great love for God, you're compelled to demonstrate evidence of your faith by exemplifying each fruit . . . by tonight . . . which is impossible!

Author Wade Goodall wrote in *The Fruit of the Spirit*:
> As we avoid sin and sincerely desire to be led by the Spirit, we will experience steady growth in patience. We will become less angry (or hostile) and have more control over what we say. Our life will seem calmer. When we find it necessary to respond assertively or to appropriately confront someone, we will be in control. The Holy Spirit will help us with our sense of timing as we determine when (or if) we need to say or do something. This maturity doesn't come overnight: God will help us develop new habits as we grow in relationship with Him.

In this way, we don't get the fruit of the Spirit; rather, the fruit of the Spirit gets us.

God has given us the Holy Spirit to help us mature in Christ and yield fruit. Read Galatians 5:16. Circle the word that best fits this sentence.

Die   Walk   Hide   in/by the Spirit and it will be more difficult to sin.

In the context of our verse, *walk* is defined as "a continued mode of conduct or behavior." In fact, the infinitive "to walk" can be translated "to live."

The NLT paraphrases Galatians 5:16 this way: **Let the Holy Spirit guide our lives.**

What are some ways you can walk with God?

An actor interviewed on the *Good Morning America* television show was asked how he prepared for a movie role. He answered, "You start to feel more like the character and think like he would, the more you spend time with him."

While the actor was referring to time spent as the person he is portraying, the implication for Christians is the same: We need to spend time with God to understand His character.

How important to you is your time spent alone with God?

Read on to Galatians 5:17. The Spirit is in direct opposition to _____.

Sinful human nature, called the flesh, is contrary to the Spirit and doesn't produce spiritual fruit.

Galatians 5:19–21 reveals evidences of being in the flesh.

Notes

List them here:

_____ _____ _____
_____ _____ _____
_____ _____ _____
_____ _____ _____
_____ _____ _____

This passage ends with the words *and things like these*.

Our flesh naturally desires sin. To fight against what we naturally desire, we must be led by the Spirit.

Refer to the fruit of the Spirit list. Which one(s) listed come(s) more easily for you?

What does Galatians 5:24 tell us to do with sinful behavior?

How would you describe the term "crucify"?

No matter how we say it, we need to get rid of the practice of sin.

In Galatians 2:20 Paul tells us this: *I have been crucified with Christ. It is no longer I who live, but Christ who lives in me. And the life I now live in the flesh I live by faith in the Son of God, who loved me and gave himself for me* (ESV).

You may want to write the opposite of each spiritual fruit to answer this next question.

What sinful attitude is the most difficult for you to crucify?

Second Corinthians 5:17 tells us *if anyone is in Christ, he is a new creature; the old things passed away; behold, new things have come.*

Letting go of old behaviors can be difficult, especially when they're something that brings temporary satisfaction.

What does "old things passed away" mean to you?

What are new things?

Producing fruit takes time. While we walk with God daily, old behaviors begin to diminish and new behaviors emerge.

Mature fruit is always connected to the vine. Read John 15:1. Who is the True Vine we connect to? _____

Once when I was picking tomatoes from the vine, I reached for what appeared to be a gorgeous plump tomato screaming to be eaten on a sandwich. But when I got closer, I found it was rotten. The tomato had become separated from the vine and was squashed against the ground.

Sometimes the fruit we produce is rotten. Like the tomato, we attach ourselves to something other than the True Vine. When we attach ourselves to the sinful flesh of the world, we begin to smell like our rotten culture. We might appear beautiful on the outside, but inside we're rotten.

Read John 15:2–4. Why is pruning necessary?

When God cuts away unproductive branches, such as a sinful habit or a selfish attitude, new growth springs forth. Sometimes God's pruning cuts away something that will hurt us. C. S. Lewis wrote, "God will work off our rough edges by rubbing us up against

Notes

tough experiences and people."[17] Other times, He's equipping us for a specific task, event, or relationship. He uses people and circumstances in our lives as a means to prune us.

When have you felt the painful effects of God's pruning tools? What was the result? What do you believe God is cutting from you?

Henry Wingblade wrote in *The Fruit of the Spirit"*

> The Christian personality is hidden deep inside us. It is unseen, like the soup carried in a tureen high over a waiter's head. No one knows what's inside — unless the waiter is bumped and trips! Just so, people don't know what's inside us until we've been bumped. But if Christ is living inside, what spills out is the fruit of the Spirit.[18]

If you were bumped, what would spill out of you today?

What would you like to spill out?

Matthew 7:15–20 tells us *every good tree bears good fruit, but a bad tree bears bad fruit. A good tree cannot bear bad fruit, and a bad tree cannot bear good fruit* (NIV).

John Bunyan, author of *Pilgrim's Progress* wrote:

> If my life is fruitless, it doesn't matter who praises me, and if my life is fruitful, it doesn't matter who criticizes me." God takes responsibility for producing spiritual fruit when we surrender our lives to Him.

Then, like the evidence in Will's pocket, we'll have evidence of Christ living and shining in us.

What Meant the Most to You from Today's Study?   *Notes*

Application

- Purchase fruit magnets at a kitchen supply store. Using a permanent marker write the spiritual fruit — one on each magnet. Put these on your refrigerator or filing cabinet or any other place that holds magnets to remind you of the beautiful fruit God is producing in you.

- Read Kyle Idleman's book *Not a Fan*.

- Listen to "Changed" by Jordan Feliz
https://www.youtube.com/watch?v=BGPMX4zU9jc

Light from the Scriptures

Since you have been raised to new life with Christ, set your sights on the realities of heaven, where Christ sits in the place of honor at God's right hand. Think about the things of heaven, not the things of earth. For you died to this life, and your real life is hidden with Christ in God. And when Christ, who is your life, is revealed to the whole world, you will share in all His glory. So put to death the sinful, earthly things lurking within you. Have nothing to do with sexual immorality, impurity, lust, and evil desires. Don't be greedy, for a greedy person is an idolater, worshiping the things of this world. Because of these sins, the anger of God is coming. You used to do these things when your life was still part of this world. But now is the time to get rid of anger, rage, malicious behavior, slander, and dirty language. Don't lie to each other, for you have stripped off your old sinful nature and all its wicked deeds. Put on your new nature, and be renewed as you learn to know your Creator and become like Him. In this new life, it doesn't matter if you are a Jew or a Gentile, circumcised or uncircumcised, barbaric, uncivilized, slave, or free. Christ is all that matters, and He lives in all of us.

Colossians 3:1–11 NLT

> We don't get the fruit of the Spirit; rather, the fruit of the Spirit gets us.

Notes

Focus:
We shine
brightly
in the midst
of darkness.

❧ 7 ☙
Shining Through the Storm

God permits what He hates, to accomplish that which He loves.

~ Joni Erikson Tada
Author and Founder of Joni and Friends, Quadriplegic

It was 9 a.m. at the beachfront condo and already hot, despite it being the beginning of autumn. With three pools and lots of empty chairs, it might have seemed strange that I would plop down right next to the only occupied lounger. I guessed the lounger belonged to the woman who was swimming. Within five minutes, she got out of the pool.

"I'm sorry to have crowded your space," I said to the older woman. "It was the only place in the shade."

She proceeded to dry off and stretch. "That's okay. I don't blame you. This is a good spot with a nice breeze."

My Bible was open on my lap, and I was holding a Bible study with my right hand. My eyes were swollen and wet from tears. Despite my sorrow, I looked her straight in the eye and smiled.

"It looks like you're studying," she continued.

"Yes, I am. Are you familiar with this study?" She glanced down at my Bible and accompanying Bible study book and responded, "Oh no . . . I'm an agnostic."

I knew what that meant, but I wanted to hear it from her. "What does that mean?"

She flung her hands in the air and said, "Don't know . . . don't care."

I nodded and continued to smile. "Yeah . . . I believe God created me for a purpose, but I'm experiencing some tough stuff right now. I've gotten bad news, so I'm reading my Bible and searching for hope."

She continued to dry her back but looked deep into my tear-stained face. "You radiate," she said. "You're the kind of Christian Jesus was talking about."

With those words, she said goodbye and walked away. I sat stunned. *She knew how Jesus defined Christians?*

This woman who claimed to be an agnostic saw Jesus shining through the cracks of my brokenness. A woman who claimed she didn't know or care about His existence said, "I see Jesus in you."

I'm not sure who the moment was for. Would this woman one day need hope and remember our encounter, or was this encouragement for me during a dark moment?

Dark seasons are inevitable:

- Broken relationships
- Stressful situations, decisions, and work
- Disappointments
- Financial upsets
- Health issues
- Consequences of poor decisions

Maybe you've experienced one or more of these. Or perhaps your trouble isn't on the list. Think about when you went through a dark season. We'll come back to it in a bit.

Trouble has many names: Affliction, adversity, trials, and storms are just a few. Regardless of the names we use, they all represent pain.

Emotional storms have the potential to shake our foundation. We're whisked away by the surge of emotion. Everything we thought we knew or depended on suddenly becomes foreign. The hailstorms pound our hearts and minds. Hurricane-force storms change the landscape of our circumstances. Other storms are likened to a heavy rainstorm that keeps us inside all day. We fear we'll snap in two like the mountain trees. Sometimes our storm resembles heavy mountain snow, pressing against our back. We think we'll be crushed under the weight of our burdens.

James, who most Bible scholars say is the half-brother of Jesus, wrote to believers in the New Testament church. Read James 1:2–4 and fill in the missing words:

Consider it all joy, my brethren, _____ you encounter various _____, knowing that the testing of your faith produces endurance. And let endurance have its perfect result, so that you may be perfect and complete, lacking in nothing.

Notes

Did you write *when* and *trials*? The KJV uses the term *divers temptation* — or various types of temptation — in place of *trials*. We may think of temptation as coming from the devil as he tempts us to do what we think will bring us pleasure. But a person can also be tempted to worry, fear, or doubt God's love.

Three New Testament Greek words are used for *trial*:

Purosis alludes to going through the fires of suffering for the purpose of refining one's character.[19]

Perirasmos implies God is testing our commitment. Will we remain faithful to Him, or will we give in to temptation and sin?[20]

Dokimion is used in reference to proving one's faith is genuine. After being tested, our faith remains.[21]

Let's briefly examine the trials that Job, Joseph, and David experienced.

Read Job 1:1. How is Job described?

God allowed Job to lose his family, his possessions, his health, and to suffer false accusations (Job 1:6–22, 2:1–10). Job's friends counseled him with what sounded logical, but it wasn't godly counsel. As a matter of fact, their advice was from Satan. Satan came to Eliphaz at night (Job 4:15–21) and whispered the counsel to give to Job later.

Read Job 1:20. What was Job's response to his storm?

Read Job 1:22. Job remained _____
_____.

Look back at the Greek words for trial. Which of the three types of trials do you think Job suffered?

Joseph's story is summarized in Genesis chapters 37–50. Joseph endured suffering over a span of approximately thirteen years and faced many trials and temptations during that period. Each time, he escaped temptation. He emerged as a faithful follower of God with integrity and character. God didn't waste Joseph's suffering, and He won't waste ours either. God used Joseph's experiences to equip him to become second in command under pharaoh.

Read Genesis 50:20. What did Joseph say to his brothers after they were reunited?

Which Greek word would you use to describe Joseph's trials?

Known as "a man after God's own heart" David went from shepherd boy to king. In his journey, he suffered numerous trials. His affair with Bathsheba led to a pregnancy. As a cover up, David conspired to have Bathsheba's husband killed. He spent the next year avoiding God in an effort to hide his sin. The consequences were severe. David's sin caused long-term suffering and brokenness which affected his physical, emotional, and spiritual health.

Which kind of trial most likely describes David's trouble?

In God's mercy, however, that wasn't the end for David or his purpose. Read 2 Samuel 12:13. What did David do that enabled him to stand after the storm?

Storms serve different purposes and are as diverse and personal as the people experiencing them. Regardless, God remains faithful and uses our storms for our benefit, the benefit of others, and for His purpose. Consider a past or present trial and answer the following questions:

What did God teach you?

How did God reveal His character?

How was your faith strengthened?

Refer again to the Greek words for trial. Which of these words best describes the purpose for this particular trial?

Read Romans 8:28. What do you think it means that *"all things work together"*?

This verse isn't implying that all incidents are good — because they aren't. But collectively God uses the events in our lives to produce a good outcome. God wants to bless us and will go to great lengths to do so.

For example, meteorologists describe the eye of a hurricane — its center — as peaceful. In our storms, centering our thoughts and focusing on Jesus protects us from anxiety and keeps us in peace . . . even if it means re-centering every hour.

When we stay tethered to God's Word, the storms won't destroy us. God doesn't use words in a careless way. He tells us in Psalm 92:12: *The righteous will flourish like a palm tree*. During tropical storms and hurricanes, palm trees bend to protect themselves. When the storm is over, they stand tall again.

We flourish like a palm tree because we bend:

- our knees in prayer.
- our independence and self-reliance and humbly ask God to intervene.
- down in a kneeling position and seek protection from God.

Read Hebrews 6:19 and fill in the missing word: *This hope we have as an _____ of the soul. Jesus is our hope.*

When are you most likely to put your hope in someone or something other than God?

When do you most often run to God?

Dictionary.com defines hope as "a feeling of expectation and desire for a certain thing to happen."[22] But *The Bible Dictionary* expands this definition: "Hope is the expectation of what God has promised."[23] He has promised to be faithful and provide all we need.

Match the following verses to their reference. It's okay if you're using a translation other than the NASB. You'll get the gist of the verse.

___ Isaiah 40:31   A. *After you have suffered for a little while, the God of all grace, who called you to His eternal glory in Christ, will Himself perfect, confirm, strengthen and establish you.*

___ Romans 15:13   B. *Now may the God of hope fill you with all joy and peace in believing, so that you will abound in hope by the power of the Holy Spirit.*

___ 2 Corinthians 4:16–17   C. *Those who wait for the Lord will gain new strength; They will mount up with wings like eagles, they will run and not get tired, they will walk and not become weary.*

___ 1 Peter 5:10   D. *Do not lose heart, but though our outer man is decaying, yet our inner man is being renewed day by day. For momentary, light affliction is producing for us an eternal weight of glory far beyond all comparison.*

Notes

Notes

While waiting for your storm to pass, keep an eye out for the rainbow by speaking positively about the future. Say things like:

- *You who have shown me many troubles and distresses, will revive me again, and will bring me up again from the depths of the earth.* (Psalm 71:20)

- *When I walk through the Valley of Weeping it will become a place of refreshing springs where pools of blessings collect after the rain.* (Psalm 84:6 NLT)

- *When you pass through the waters, I will be with you; and when you pass through the rivers, they will not sweep over you. When you walk through the fire, you will not be burned; the flames will not set you ablaze.* (Isaiah 43:2 NIV)

We can read about God's faithfulness or we can experience it for ourselves. First hand experience matures our faith and enables us to authentically share our hope with others. Psalm 139:12 tells us this: *Even the darkness is not dark to You, And the night is as bright as the day. Darkness and light are alike to* You. In this way, even while in darkness, we reflect His light.

Second Corinthians 4:8–9 tells us: *We are afflicted in every way, but not crushed; perplexed, but not despairing; persecuted, but not forsaken; struck down, but not destroyed.*

Based on this Scripture, circle four things that won't happen to the woman who is steadfast in her faith during adversity. Storms help mature our faith, gain godly perspective, and help us trust God more as He transforms us into His image.

Back to our opening story: Sometimes I wonder if I'll see this self-proclaimed agnostic in heaven. Wouldn't it be wonderful if she'll see me and say, "I was in a deep, terrible trial and needed hope. I remembered you gathered hope by reading the Bible. I tried it . . . and found Jesus."

Our suffering isn't wasted. There is purpose in our pain. Shine on!

What Meant the Most to You from Today's Study?   *Notes*

Application

- In storms, continue to make a list of things you're thankful for.
- Ease your emotions by putting on praise music and worship the Lord Jesus Christ.
- Read Beth Moore's book *Get out of that Pit*.
- Listen to "It Is Well with My Soul." The hymn was written by Horatio G. Spafford while he faced his own personal storm. https://www.youtube.com/watch?v=8tdoWK34lpc

As we experience God's faithfulness firsthand, our faith will mature and enable us to authentically share our hope with others.

Light from the Scriptures

When I am afraid, I will put my trust in You. In God, whose word I praise, In God I have put my trust; I shall not be afraid. What can mere man do to me? All day long they distort my words; All their thoughts are against me for evil. They attack, they lurk, they watch my steps, as they have waited to take my life. Because of wickedness, cast them forth, In anger put down the peoples, O God! You have taken account of my wanderings; Put my tears in Your bottle. Are they not in Your book? Then my enemies will turn back in the day when I call; This I know, that God is for me. In God, whose word I praise, In the LORD, whose word I praise, in God I have put my trust, I shall not be afraid. What can man do to me?

Psalm 56:3–11

❦ 8 ❦
With Eyes Wide Open

When the Lord makes it clear you're to follow Him in this new direction, focus fully on Him and refuse to be distracted by comparisons with others.

~ Charles R. Swindoll
Author and Pastor

Focus: We shine when we keep our eyes on Jesus.

> MORE THAN THIRTY YEARS AGO, MY HUSBAND AND I WENT skiing. I was eager to learn, and he was confident in his ability to teach me. After arriving at the ski resort, we got my skis and boots and headed to the beginner's slope so I could get comfortable being on skis. Soon though, we ventured over to the ski lift for a ride up the mountain. Evergreens lined the trail of white against the backdrop of a sparkling blue sky. Swift skiers down below made the experience look easy and enjoyable.
>
> But the beauty went unnoticed the moment I slipped off the ski lift bottom first. My husband graciously lifted me up. I gazed down from the top of the mountain, which seemed to have no end. Terror welled in my chest, and tears blurred my vision. I was frozen with fear.
>
> My husband skied backwards down the mountain holding my hands, slowly pulling me along. But my eyes focused on the surroundings. Watching the other accomplished skiers distracted me. They were fast, graceful, and talented.
>
> I felt silly, incapable, and hopeless.
>
> Comparing myself to others, led to unexpected defeat.

The word *compare* is defined this way: "to examine the character or qualities of, especially in order to discover resemblances or differences."[24]

Certain comparisons are observations that help us acquire knowledge, such as saying, "That object is red, and this one is blue." Unhealthy comparisons of ourselves to others cause us to feel eclipsed by brighter, shining light. We see others' lights as livelier, more intense, and much more brilliant; in our estimation, they overshadow our own light. We sense our light becoming dim. Then we make the assumption: We're not as capable.

Look at the list below. Have you made comparisons between yourself and someone else in these areas? If so, which ones?

- organizational skills
- fashion choices
- your children's behaviors
- intelligence
- godliness or spiritual maturity
- physical appearance or health
- marital status or stability
- career opportunities or satisfaction
- ministry success
- financial status
- Other _____

Which comparison, if any, is a current obstacle for you?

Sometimes comparisons sneak up on us in a surprising way when we think, *I wish God would do in my life what He's doing in hers. I wish I was as effective. I wish I had her gifts and talents.*

On the ski slope, my eyes were drawn to the more competent skiers. I took my focus off of my husband. I didn't apply what I had learned to do on the beginner's slope. Instead, I focused on what I couldn't do. As I lost sight of the intended outcome — to joyfully arrive at the bottom of the mountain — fear, hopelessness, and the more talented skiers became my obstacles.

Hannah More, 18th century English religious writer, summed up why we might be blinded by obstacles. "Obstacles are those frightening things you see when you take your eyes off the goal."[25]

Notes

Do you have goals? If so, what are they? If you don't have goals, what is keeping you from making them?

Hebrews 12:2 teaches us what we need to do with our eyes. Read this verse and fill in the blank.

_____ *my eyes on Jesus.*

Depending on your translation, words include: *fix, look, keep.*

Read 2 Corinthians 4:18. What do you think it means to look at "things which are not seen"?

To trust beyond what we can see indicates we give attention to what's eternal, such as the hope we cling to when we're desperate, the wisdom we acquire after seeking God, the faith needed to be still and let God work and move in powerful ways, and the strength to move when God prompts us to go.

Paul wrote in Colossians 3:2: *Set your mind on the things above, not on the things that are on this earth.*

How do you define "things above"?

"Things above" is the motivation behind worthy deeds and aspirations; Christ-honoring ideas and actions promoting God's kingdom; endeavors and achievements that are sustained by God and bring Him glory. Things above have higher purposes.

What's easy about this mind-set? What's difficult?

How are these things different from what we see on earth?

Notes

We must close our spiritual eyes to negative comparisons and open our eyes to God's truth. (See chapter one.) This will enable us to be victorious.

Satan's wicked strategies include attacking our minds. Recall John 10:10. What three things does the devil yearn to do?

How does the devil use comparisons to steal our purpose, kill our dreams, and destroy our self-image?

Which of the following emotions has the devil used on you in the past or is using on you now? Circle all that apply.

- Insecurity
- Jealousy/Envy
- Unworthiness
- Fear
- Hopelessness
- Incapability
- Ineffectiveness
- Other _____

In what ways can comparing one's self to others also lead to a grandiose opinion?

How does social media promote comparisons?

How can social media influence how you feel about yourself?

Notes

Social media didn't jumpstart the comparison game. Judgments and opinions have been part of our nature since the fall of mankind back in Genesis. But we've seen how social media can lead to jealousy, discouragement, discontentment, and pride. Match the following comparison account to the reference in Scripture:

    __ Genesis 30:1   A. Pride/Arrogance

    __ 1 Samuel 18:18–19   B. Jealousy and Worthlessness

    __ Luke 18:9–14   C. Competition

What lie have you believed:

About yourself?

Your goals?

Your purpose?

The small, but significant things you do?

Surprisingly, last year I relived my ski experience in a dream. This time there was a powerful life-changing truth.

Again, my husband was skiing backward down the mountain, holding my hands. But this time my eyes were closed. I couldn't see the difficulty of the slope or the other more skilled skiers. I focused on the end result and we finished ahead of the other skiers. The difference in the first and second trip down the slope was what I determined to focus on.

Matthew 14:22–33 reveals Peter's enlightening experience of miraculously walking on water. Where was Peter looking when he stepped out?

Look closely at Matthew 14:30. What happened when Peter took his eyes off Jesus and looked away at the raging winds surrounding Him?

The implication is powerful. Obstacles in our life may appear to be like the raging wind surrounding Peter or like a mountain — overwhelming, steep, or unattainable. Circumstances may be frightening or simply impossible. Others' accomplishments and successes leave us feeling inadequate. Silly, incapable, and hopeless. Frozen with fear.

When, if ever, have you felt this way? What was the outcome?

The difference in being paralyzed with fear or winning the race depends on who we trust to lead us and where we direct our gaze. We must intentionally shift our focus from what we can see — our insufficiency and the distractions that overwhelm us — to what we can't see — Jesus. With eyes wide open, we trust Him and hold tightly to His hands.

Read Luke 11:34. What does this verse tell us is the lamp of one's body?

When our eye is clear, our body is _____ _____.

Notes

In Ephesians 1:18 Paul tells us, *I pray that the eyes of your heart may be enlightened, so that you will know what is the hope of His calling, what are the riches of the glory of His inheritance in the saints.*

How are the eyes of one's heart different from physical sight?

Let' resist the urge to compare ourselves with others. Let's fix our eyes on Jesus and His great love that enables us to fulfill our unique purpose.

What Meant the Most to You from Today's Study?

The difference in being frozen with fear or winning the race depends on who we trust to lead us and where we direct our gaze

Application

- Write "Fix My Eyes" (Hebrews 12:2) on a sticky note and draw two big eyes. Put the note in a place you look every day, so it will remind you to focus on Him.

- Listen to "Fix My Eyes" by King and Country. https://www.youtube.com/watch?v=Yd2we03Sy4I.

Light from the Scriptures

We who are strong have an obligation to bear with the failings of the weak, and not to please ourselves. Let each of us please his neighbor for his good, to build him up. For Christ did not please himself, but as it is written, "The reproaches of those who reproached you fell on me." For whatever was written in former days was written for our instruction, that through endurance and through the encouragement of the Scriptures we might have hope. May the God of endurance and encouragement grant you to live in such harmony with one another, in accord with Christ Jesus, that together you may with one voice glorify the God and Father of our Lord Jesus Christ. Therefore welcome one another as Christ has welcomed you, for the glory of God.

Romans 15:1–7 ESV

9
God's Divine Appointment

Faith never knows where it is being led, but it loves and knows the One who is leading.

~ Oswald Chambers
My Utmost for His Highest

Focus: We shine as we fulfill our purpose.

Two life-changing events occurred when I was in the fourth grade. First, I trusted Jesus as my Savior. Second, my family took a six-week vacation and traveled to every state in the United States. My life fell apart two years later when my parents divorced and mom moved us to North Carolina — the state she deemed her favorite after vacationing there. Suddenly, I was a new student in a sixth-grade classroom. I was friendless and without a church. Loneliness and fear welcomed me to my new state.

But God had a plan. He placed a girl at the bus stop on my first day of school who "just happened" to be in my class. Friendly and kind, she invited me to church.

God's plan continued to unfold. The following year, the pastor of that church invited me to take a sign language class. I loved signing and spent the next five years interpreting for the deaf. My senior year of high school arrived, and, due to my family's financial situation, college was unaffordable, especially at the Christian college my heart longed to attend. As a last resort, I contacted my father. He agreed to pay my tuition and buy me a car if I moved back to California and attended a secular college. God whispered to my heart and led me to turn down my father's offer. I was heartbroken. College was out and I felt hopeless.

But God's plan couldn't be thwarted. Within weeks, someone from a Christian college contacted me, seeking interpreters for their deaf students. In return, I'd receive an almost full scholarship for my college education.

The devastation of a broken family, a divine appointment with a new friend, an extraordinary pastor who reached out to a teen, and the seemingly small act of learning sign language changed the trajectory of my life. The people and timing were strategic. I couldn't have known that learning sign language in seventh grade would be my ticket to a college education.

Notes

God made provision for college years before I asked. And that was just the beginning. Isaiah 65:24 became alive for me: *Before they call, I will answer; and while they are still speaking, I will hear.*

God is our Way-Maker, creating divine appointments, interruptions, and opportunities for His children to fulfill their purpose. As on a staircase, each step propels us to our next assignment. In this way, we have many purposes, and each mission is a critical foundation for the next. Our main purpose is to love God and obey Him.

Now we'll examine the unfolding of Moses' purpose. We'll finish with *your story . . . your purpose.*

Read the following passages.

Exodus 1:16. What were the midwives told to do? What was their reaction? How would you describe their view of God?

Exodus 1:18. When Pharaoh summoned the midwives and asked them why they let the male babies live, what was their response?

Exodus 1:20–21. How did God bless the midwives?

Exodus 2:2–3. After hiding Moses for three months, who placed him in the basket and into the Nile River?

Imagine all that might have happened to a baby in a basket floating down a river. What are some possible dangers God protected Moses from?

You don't have to be a mother to imagine how difficult it must have been for Moses' mother, Jochabed, to surrender her natural desires and let her baby go. What emotions might she have experienced?

What does her action say about her faith?

Exodus 2:5–6. Who discovered the baby in the river?

What was her reaction to the crying baby?

Exodus 2:7. What did Miriam, Moses' sister, suggest?

Exodus 2:9. Pharaoh's daughter agreed with Miriam's suggestion and even made an additional offer. What was it?

Are you kidding? Imagine Jochabed's delight when her baby was temporarily returned to her to be nursed and nurtured . . . and she was financially compensated!

Bible scholars believe that babies were nursed between three and seven years, with the average age being five years. This means Jochabed was granted several years with her son.[26]

What do you think she taught him?

Notes

Which of the following may he have been taught?

love for God   bravery   mercy   kindness   Hebrew traditions

God had a purpose and plan for Moses. The seemingly coincidental discovery at the river changed the direction of Moses' life. The people and timing were strategic.

God is doing the same for you.

For starters, let's go straight to God's Word and examine what may be a familiar verse. Read Jeremiah 29:11 and write in your name on the blank:

I know the plans I have for you, _____, declares the Lord, plans to prosper you and not to harm you, plans to give you hope and a future. (NIV)

On a scale of 1–10, with 10 being very sure, how much do you believe this verse applies to you? _____

At times many of us wonder, *Is this all there is? Am I doing what I am supposed to be doing? Does the close of one chapter mean the end of a purposed-filled life?* Maybe a series of mistakes or mishaps has prompted you to doubt God's plan.

Let's switch gears, and do what Psalm 111:2 tells us to do: Study and ponder how God has worked in your life.

Reflect on your past. Identify times, seasons, and people where God orchestrated divine appointments and connections.

When was it difficult to obey God's leading?

How did God prepare you with the necessary skills to endure a hardship, carry a burden, or take a stance on a difficult issue?

Read Hebrews 13:21 and fill in the blank:

[God will] _____ you in every good thing to do His will, working in us that which is pleasing in His sight, through Jesus Christ, to whom be the glory forever and ever.

Most translations us the word *equip*, which is defined this way: "to provide a person, object, or place, with the thing needed for a particular purpose."[27]

God provided me with a skill that would pay for my college education, a necessary step in my journey to becoming a teacher. God provided Moses, in his early years, with a family who loved God. And God provided him with all the skills needed to lead the Hebrew people out of bondage when he was an adult.

How has He equipped you?

What are you passionate about? What are your dreams? What are your strengths and skills?

These talents are God-given and enable you to do what He has planned for you.

Reflect on a painful season. What did you gain from the experience? How did the lessons prepare you for your next step on the staircase of your purpose?

What people did God placed in your life to help accomplish His purpose?

Notes

Notes

Difficult people come into our life for two reasons: so we might influence them or they might help change us. How did difficult people motivate you to seek God?

In Psalm 77:11 the psalmist tells us, *I shall remember the deeds of the LORD; Surely I will remember Your wonders of old.*

When did God part your waters? By recalling God's past faithfulness, you'll have hope for your future, especially when you're in a waiting period. Moses left Egypt when he was forty years old; he led the Israelites out of bondage at eighty years old. Forty years of waiting prepared Moses for the leadership role God gave him.

After escaping the fury of the pharaoh, the Israelites traveled into the desert. Although they witnessed the power of God, they soon began to whine, grumble, and complain. Their sin had grave consequences. Instead of the intended eleven-day journey (Deuteronomy 1:2) to the Promised Land, the people wandered forty years in the desert.

Maybe right now, you feel God's not listening to your prayers.

While student teaching, I was unable to interpret for the deaf students and therefore acquired a small college loan to pay for my last semester. After graduation, I was hired as a teacher in a tough school with challenging circumstances and demanding people. I grumbled and complained to God. For five years, I begged God to move me. When He didn't, I wondered if He cared or was even listening.

Five years later, though, I was pleasantly surprised when I learned that because I was positioned in this work environment, my college loan had been forgiven. I was financially free. Additionally, while waiting, I learned to pray for the staff and my families. I sought God for compassion, guidance, and the strength to respond to others in a Christlike manner — necessary skills for interacting with people.

Maybe you know God is listening, but there's chaos in your life, either brought on by your choices or by someone else's.

Fear, worry, and anxious thoughts gripped my heart at the thought of my younger daughter starting high school. The effects of teen drama were still too fresh from my older daughter's experience. The summer prior to my younger daughter going to high school, she and I had an honest conversation about friendships, peer pressure, and accountability. She suggested that we start a Bible study that summer with her closest friends. Unable to find a teen study, I wrote my own. That study was published, and now we use it in the annual Shine! Conference I direct for teen girls.

We may not understand at the time what God is doing in our lives. But He has a plan. He always has a plan.

Maybe you're new to the Christian faith, or circumstances kept you wandering in your personal desert. You may feel God could never fix your situation, redeem it, or use it. This lie contradicts what God says. Write your name on the blank lines in the brackets in the following verses:

Isaiah 43:18–19. *[_____], Forget all that – it is nothing compared to what I am going to do. For I am about to do something new. See, I have already begun! Do you not see it? I will make a pathway through the wilderness. I will create rivers in the dry wasteland* (NLT).

Lamentations 3:22–23. *The* L<small>ORD</small>*'s lovingkindnesses indeed never cease, [_____], For His compassions never fail. They are new every morning; Great is Your faithfulness.*

Isaiah 41:10. *Do not fear, [_____], for I am with you; Do not anxiously look about you, for I am your God. I will strengthen you, surely I will help you, Surely I will uphold you with My righteous right hand.*

1 John 1:9. *If [_____] confess[es] [her] sins, He is faithful and just and will forgive [_____ 's] sins and purify [_____] from all unrighteousness.* (NIV)

Notes

Notes

Regardless of the steps we're climbing, we can hold on to the hope that God is faithfully revealing His plan a bit at a time. Start or continue to:

- Talk to God. Believe Him when He says He created you for a purpose. Then obey what He tells you to do, even when it doesn't make sense.

- Believe that God works all things together for your good. He takes your mistakes and brings something valuable from them.

- Read God's Word and do what He says. Proverbs 4:26 tells us, *Watch the path of your feet and all your ways will be established.* The KJV uses the word *ponder* for watch. Think about what you're doing and where you're going. Eliminate opportunities that go against God's Word. Proverbs 3:5–6 says, *Trust in the Lord with all your heart and do not lean on your own understanding. In all your ways acknowledge Him, and He will make your paths straight.*

- Establish friendships with people who keep you accountable, pray for you, and help move you closer to understanding your purpose.

God prepared and led Moses. And God will continue to prepare and lead you and me. Will we be as trusting as Jochabed was, and put all our gifts, talents, hopes, and dreams into the basket? Believe what Job 22:28 tells us, *You will also decree a thing, and it will be established for you; And light will shine on your ways.*

What Meant the Most to You from Today's Study?

Application

- Take a Spiritual Gifts test. The following link is easy to use. Plan about thirty minutes to complete it. http://www.lifeway.com/lwc/files/lwcF_MYCS_030526_Spiritual_Gifts_Survey.pdf
- Read Rick Warren's book *The Purpose Driven Life*.
- Listen to "Chain Breaker" by Zach Williams https://www.youtube.com/watch?v=JGYjKR69M6U

Light from the Scriptures

David spoke the words of this song to the Lord in the day that the Lord delivered him from the hand of all his enemies and from the hand of Saul. He said, "The Lord is my rock and my fortress and my deliverer; My God, my rock, in whom I take refuge, My shield and the horn of my salvation, my stronghold and my refuge; My savior, You save me from violence. "I call upon the Lord, who is worthy to be praised, And I am saved from my enemies."

2 Samuel 22:1–4

Notes

God is our Way-Maker, creating divine appointments, interruptions, and opportunities for His children to fulfill their purpose. As on a staircase, each step propels us to our next assignment.

Notes

*Focus:
We shine when we're prepared to fight.*

✥ 10 ✥
Spiritual Warfare

I'm not afraid of the devil. The devil can handle me – he's got judo I never heard of. But he can't handle the One to whom I'm joined; he can't handle the One to whom I'm united; he can't handle the One whose nature dwells in my nature.

~ A. W. Tozer

> CLOTHED IN CAMOUFLAGE, BOOTS, AND HOLSTER, WILL SAT motionless perched in his favorite evergreen. The bandanna he wore around his face hid his freckles, and the hard cap covered his curly red hair. Cautiously, he emerged from behind the shadowy branches and made his way down the tree. With wooden dagger in one hand and toy rifle in the other, Will zigzagged across the grass and through a narrow strip of woods. He darted behind trees and froze. Having reached his goal, he hid beneath a large azalea bush. He watched. The six-year old soldier was protecting his home.

While observing Will at play, I realized he had prepared for battle by dressing in camouflage, boots, and a hard hat. A wooden dagger and toy rifle were his weapons. He moved with intent, carefully planning his steps.

Will faced imaginary battles. We face spiritual battles — every day — and it's essential we put on our armor.

One way Satan attempts to defeat us, is through our emotions.

On the next page, which of the following have you experienced?

Circle any that apply.

> Notes

Discouragement	Defeat	Hopelessness
Feeling Unworthy	Feeling Unloved	Feeling Overwhelmed
Insecurity	Fear	Disappointment
Worry	Dissatisfaction	Confusion
Exhaustion	Anger	Guilt/Shame
Inadequacy	Arrogance	Pride
Independence	Temptation	Depression
Anxiousness	Feeling Stuck	Other _____

How would you describe your current emotional state? If it's negative, be encouraged that God has equipped you to overcome.

How can our emotional state affect the ways in which we make decisions?

Read Ephesians 6:11 and fill in the missing words. *Put on the full armor of God, so that you will be able to stand firm against the _____ _____ .*

Anything contrary to God's Word is a lie and an attempt by Satan to destroy us and our testimony. We must be prepared for his attack. In the verse above, circle the words "put on." To "put on" is an action — something that we do. Covering our bodies in spiritual armor, as a soldier does, indicates we're going into battle.

Ephesians 6:14–17 tells us: *Stand firm then, with the belt of truth buckled around your waist, with the breastplate of righteousness in place, and with your feet fitted with the readiness that comes from the gospel of peace. In addition to all this, take up the shield of faith, with which you can extinguish all the flaming arrows of the evil one. Take the helmet of salvation and the sword of the Spirit, which is the Word of God.* (NIV)

Notes

In the previous verses, circle the pieces of armor required.

Battle gear has its specific purpose.

Belt of Truth	An offensive weapon that attacks with truth.
Breastplate of Righteousness	Worn in battle to protect the heart and vital organs.
Feet Fitted with Readiness	Enables us to be vigilant.
Shield of Faith	Deflects the flaming arrows of the devil.
Helmet of Salvation	Protects our thoughts. The assurance of salvation is our defense against anything Satan throws at us.
Sword of the Spirit	God's Word teaches us.

Truth is found in the Holy Bible. It's imperative we know what's written in the Bible if we're going to be able to fight the devil's attack on our emotions or circumstances. Gaining truth through teaching and divine discipline yields *righteousness*. Our physical *feet* go where our thoughts and desires tell them to go. Read Proverbs 4:26 and fill in the missing word.

_____the path of your feet and all your ways will be established.

Depending on your translation you may have written the words: give *careful thought* (NIV), *ponder* (KJV, NKJV, ESV) or *watch* (NASB).

Ponder is defined as "to think about or reflect on."[28] We think about our choices and actions and determine if they are leading us down a path of success in God's eyes.

As our **faith** grows, we'll learn to trust God more and want what He wants for us. Our desires will align with His — that's a sure way to regularly defeat the devil. And because we have **salvation**, ultimately the devil has already been defeated. The helmet we put over our head will protect us from anything that's contrary to God's truth. God's Word is a **sword** which we use to kill the lies of the Enemy.

Jesus is always our example. Read Matthew 4:1–11. Describe the armor Jesus used to fight Satan's attack.

Hebrews 4:12 tells us *the Word of God is living and active and sharper than any two-edged sword, and piercing as far as the division of soul and spirit, of both joints and marrow, and able to judge the thoughts and intentions of the heart.*

How can we prepare to use the defense Jesus used?

What strategies do you take to help you understand God's Word?

Paul tells us in 1 Corinthians 2:14 that *a natural man does not accept the things of the Spirit of God, for they are foolishness to him; and he cannot understand them, because they are spiritually appraised.*

So then, what good is the Bible if we can't understand it? Author and pastor John Piper sheds light on this question:

> Natural people are defined here as people who do not have God's Spirit. They are simply ordinary people whose hearts and minds are not touched with the renewing work of the Holy Spirit. The opposite of "natural man" is "spiritual man" — a person whose mind and heart are renewed by the Spirit . . . In verse 14 the "natural man" cannot understand the "things of the Spirit of God" because they are "spiritually discerned." Paul is able to understand them because he has received the Spirit. Therefore, a "natural person" is a person who has not received the Spirit. That's why he can't understand "the things of the Spirit of God."[29]

That should be sweet encouragement. Understanding God's Word and using it as our defense is not solely dependent upon our intelligence or reading level. The Holy Spirit interprets Scripture and leads us to understanding.

How often do you suit up for your battles? Circle one.

        Daily   Weekly   Monthly

The scriptures on the following pages are God's truth. Use them to fight whatever fiery dart Satan is hurling toward you today. To make it more personal, write your name on the blank line.

When Satan attacks us with:	God says:
Discouragement	The Lord is the one who goes ahead of you; He will be with [_____]. He will not fail you or forsake you. Do not fear or be dismayed. Deuteronomy 31:8
Guilt and shame	He will again have compassion on [_____]; He will tread [her] iniquities under foot. Yes, You will cast all [her] sins into the depths of the sea. Micah 7:19
	If [_____] confess our sins, He is faithful and righteous to forgive us our sins and to cleanse us from all unrighteousness. John 1:9
Hopelessness	Now may the God of hope fill you [_____] with all joy and peace in believing, so that you will abound in hope by the power of the Holy Spirit. Romans 15:13
Fear and Worry	Peace I leave with you [_____]; My peace I give to you; not as the world gives do I give to you. Do not let your heart be troubled, nor let it be fearful. John 14:27
Inadequacy	The Lord gives wisdom [to _____]; From His mouth come knowledge and understanding. Proverbs 2:6
Feeling Unloved and Unworthy	I have loved you with an everlasting love [_____]; Therefore I have drawn you with lovingkindness. Jeremiah 31:3
Confusion	God is not the author of confusion, [_____], but of peace. 1 Corinthians 14:33 (NKJV)
Disappointment/Defeat	Let us not lose heart in doing good, for in due time [_____] will reap if [she does] not grow weary. Galatians 6:9

Exhaustion — [_____], who hope[s] in the LORD will renew [her] strength. [She] will soar on wings like eagles; [she] will run and not grow weary, [she] will walk and not be faint. Isaiah 40:31 (NIV)

Pride/Arrogance — He gives us more grace. That is why Scripture says: "God opposes the proud, [_____], but shows favor to the humble." James 4:6 (NIV)

Anger — [_____] must be quick to hear, slow to speak and slow to anger; for the anger of man does not achieve the righteousness of God. James 1:19–20

Dissatisfaction — I [_____] have learned to be content in whatever circumstances I am. Philippians 4:11

Independence — I am continually with You [_____]; You have taken hold of my right hand. Psalm 73:23

Temptation — The temptations in [_____]'s life are no different from what others experience. And God is faithful. He will not allow the temptation to be more than you, [_____], can stand. When you are tempted, he will show you a way out so that you can endure. 1 Corinthians 10:13 (NLT)

Overwhelmed — Give all your worries and cares to God, [_____], for He cares about you. 1 Peter 5:7 (NLT)

Depression/Anxiety — When the righteous cry for help, the Lord hears and delivers them out of all their troubles. The Lord is near to the brokenhearted and saves the crushed in spirit. Many are the afflictions of the righteous, but the Lord delivers [_____] out of them. Psalm 34:17–19 (ESV)

Baffled — I will instruct you, [_____], and teach you in the way you should go; I will counsel you with my loving eye on you. Psalm 32:8 (NIV)

Notes

> Anything contradictory to God's Word is a lie and an attempt by Satan to destroy us and our testimony.

In Romans 13:12 Paul tells us: *Let us put aside the deeds of darkness and put on the armor of light.* (NIV). Arise . . . dress in armor and successfully defeat Satan's sabotaging tactics.

What Meant the Most to You from Today's Study?

Application

- Look back at the Scripture boxes where you wrote your name. Transfer each verse to a sticky note and place these notes on your mirror, coffee pot, refrigerator, car dashboard, or any place you will regularly see them. Read them aloud.
- Listen to "Surrounded" (*Fight my Battles*) by Michael W. Smith. https://www.youtube.com/watch?v=YBl84oZxnJ4

Light from the Scriptures

I will say of the Lord, "He is my refuge and my fortress, my God, in whom I trust." Surely he will save you from the fowler's snare and from the deadly pestilence. He will cover you with his feathers, and under his wings you will find refuge; his faithfulness will be your shield and rampart. You will not fear the terror of night, nor the arrow that flies by day, nor the pestilence that stalks in the darkness, nor the plague that destroys at midday. A thousand may fall at your side, ten thousand at your right hand, but it will not come near you. You will only observe with your eyes and see the punishment of the wicked. If you make the Most High your dwelling-even the Lord, who is my refuge-then no harm will befall you, no disaster will come near your tent. For he will command his angels concerning you to guard you in all your ways; they will lift you up in their hands, so that you will not strike your foot against a stone. You will tread upon the lion and the cobra; you will trample the great lion and the serpent. "Because he loves me," says the Lord, "I will rescue him; I will protect him, for he acknowledges my name. He will call upon me, and I will answer him; I will be with him in trouble, I will deliver him and honor him. With long life will I satisfy him and show him my salvation."

Psalm 91:1–16 NIV

❧ 11 ❧
Authentic Relationships

Piglet sidled up to Pooh from behind. "Pooh!" he whispered. "Yes, Piglet?" "Nothing," said Piglet, taking Pooh's paw. "I just wanted to be sure of you."

The House at Pooh Corner

Focus: We shine when our relationships are unified through Jesus Christ.

FOUR WOMEN DESCRIBE WHAT THEY DESIRE IN A FRIEND:

"I want a real friendship, not a surface-level friendship. I don't want someone to tell me what they think I want to hear. I want someone to tell me what I need to hear. I want someone who will hold me accountable — a friendship where we hold each other up in prayer and encouragement. I want a friendship where I can be myself, laugh, and joke around; someone to take road trips with and who is okay getting lost and calling it an adventure." Age 33

"These past four years have been the first time I've had a group of women to pray for me and share life with. For all my life, I did it alone. I didn't know what I was missing. I thought isolation was a normal part of life. But being connected to women in our church group has changed my life." Age 49

"I've had friends my entire life — lots of them. Many came for a season. Most were fun, but many were dramatic. I often found myself justifying, explaining, or seeking how not to offend someone whose feelings were easily hurt. Today, I'm seeking a friendship that is less dramatic and easier to maintain. I long for a loyal friend with whom I can pray, have mutual accountability, and enjoy a splash of fun!" Age 57

"My friendships outside of God and family are based on love, honesty, and the ability to discuss my innermost thoughts in confidence. I want a friend to communicate with me in a non-critical manner. And I want to admire her because she strives to do well." Age 75

Notes

Friendships flavor our lives because God created us for meaningful relationship with others. This doesn't imply that we're co-dependent. Rather, it supports that we weren't meant to live in isolation. Charles Stanley wrote, "Independence is a prized attribute in our culture, but biblically, it isn't a worthy aspiration. Nowhere in Scripture will you find the erroneous quote, 'God helps those who help themselves.' The very fact that the Lord formed the church — a community of believers — should tell us that He did not create people for self-sufficiency or isolation."[30]

As we age and experience all that life on this earth entails, our desires and expectations for friendship may change. Can you relate to any of the four women above? If so, which one?

Are you satisfied in your current relationships, or are you seeking something different? If you're satisfied, describe in what ways. If you're seeking, what are you searching for?

Are you an introvert who prefers a good amount of time alone, or are you the social extrovert who thrives when others are present? Can a person be simultaneously both? Explain.

Although being an introvert or extrovert may influence how we pursue friendships, it isn't a factor in forming a godly relationship. We all need accountability. We see throughout history the impact strong friendships have made. We'll look at one example in a moment. But first, let's talk about the effect high-tech society has on our relationships.

How has technology helped create an environment of isolation?

How has social media improved friendships?

In what ways does social media create superficial relationships?

Do you think people seek certain relationships to validate their worth? Explain why or why not.

Why might someone feel confident in themselves because they attract hundreds of "followers" in social media?

Hundreds of followers don't equal hundreds of loyal followers. The Bible tells us about many loyal friendships and we'll look at one example in a minute. But first, read what David wrote in Psalm 144:3–5: *Set a guard over my mouth, Lord; keep watch over the door of my lips. Do not let my heart be drawn to what is evil so that I take part in wicked deeds along with those who are evildoers; do not let me eat their delicacies. Let a righteous man strike me – that is a kindness; let him rebuke me – that is oil on my head. My head will not refuse it, for my prayer will still be against the deeds of evildoers.*

List what David was asking God for.

In what ways does a friend offer *help, strength, discipline, loyalty,* and *accountability*?

Notes

The Bible tells us that David and Jonathan were faithful friends. Jonathan's father was King Saul, making Jonathan the rightful heir to the throne. But Jonathan loved God and listened to Him. When Saul began to do evil — became jealous of David and sought to kill him — Jonathan proteccted David. He knew David was God's appointed king, and warned David of his father's attacks. The Bible tells us that David and Jonathan loved each other like brothers. (Read more about their friendship in 1 Samuel 18–23.)

There are different kinds of relationships. Some are casual and less personal. Where would you find this kind of relationship?

As we get to know a person better, we may discover faulty morals or problematic situations. Has there ever been a time when you felt you needed to pull away from a relationship? If so, what compelled you?

What warning does 1 Corinthians 15:33 give?

Sometimes relationships begin within a group of people who pray together. Groups like this are often formed within a church or community setting. Praying together can fuel a special bond. Do you have relationships like these? If so, who are the people you pray with?

Your deepest, strongest, and most intimate relationships are your "core" friends. Studies on friendships conclude that the average person has a core group of friends who can be counted on one hand. The implication isn't that we don't know a lot of people or have incredible associations; rather, core friends are people we invite into our personal lives.

Who do you consider to be your core friends?

From the classic tale, *Pooh's Grand Adventure: The Search for Christopher Robin*, Christopher tells Pooh, "Promise me you'll always remember: You're braver than you believe, stronger than you seem, and smarter than you think."

Who can you count on to give you this Winnie-the-Pooh-like encouragement?

In what ways do you reciprocate?

Core friends have our best interests in mind. They lift us up, affirm our dreams and passions, encourage us to persevere, and generally inspire us. We laugh and cry with these friends. These friends want to see us shine! They point out our great traits to others and speak well of us. They have confidence in us when we have none. These are the rarest and the most treasured relationships.

Specific ingredients are necessary for successful core relationships: respect, love, forgiveness, loyalty, edification, and reciprocation. A general definition of each of these six words follows:[31]

Respect:	a concern for someone or something; a high regard; courtesy
Love:	a love that is kind, strong, and constant; there's an affection for and dedication to another
Forgiveness:	giving up resentment of or claim to requital; granting relief from payment; to cease to feel resentment against

Loyalty: faithful in allegiance

Edification: to instruct and improve especially in moral and religious knowledge

Reciprocation: shared, felt, or shown by both sides

Respect

The foundation of a godly friendship is built on the mutual foundation of Christ. Aside from this, there may be differences (probably are) in the friendship. One friend may be quieter in a group setting, while the other gets involved in conversation. One may like sports, while the other enjoys crafts. These differences make us unique. Genuine, core friends value these differences. They show respect even when there's a difference of opinion.

Has there ever been a time when a friend did not respect you? What impact did it have on the friendship?

What is one thing you and your core friend disagree on?

How do you make the relationship work?

Love

The mutual thread of love for God is woven into the fabric of a Christian's core friendships. David and Jonathan had in common their faith and love for God. They swore their oath of friendship in the name of Jehovah (1 Samuel 20:41–42). Obedience to God was a top priority for both men.

When friends have a mutual love for God, they seek God's direction when their friend needs advice. Our closest friends are like-minded in morals and values.

From whom do you seek advice?

How does this friend hold you accountable to Christian values and truths?

How does this friend challenge you to grow spiritually?

How does this friend help you obey biblical principles?

Have you ever cried with a friend? Have you ever cried over a friend? What's the difference?

Forgiveness

Because nobody is perfect, there will be times when forgiveness is necessary.

Colossians 3:13 (NKJV) tells us this: *Bearing with one another, and forgiving one another, if anyone has a complaint against another; even as Christ forgave you, so you also must do.*

Reflect on a time when forgiveness was necessary in your relationship. What lesson did you gain?

Notes

Forgiveness may be difficult. Where do you get your strength?

Was there a time you couldn't forgive? If so, when?

When did your friend forgive you?

Loyalty

Read Proverbs 18:24. Who sticks closer than a brother?

If you're unclear on that answer, a *Nelson's NKJV Study Bible* footnote gives this insight:

> This is a difficult verse to translate because of confusion over an ambiguous Hebrew word translated here as "be friendly." This translation takes it to mean "to make oneself pleasing" as in 1 Samuel 29:4. To have friends one must be friendly. But the word could also mean "to beat each other up" as in Isaiah 24:19. Then the verse could be translated, "Sometimes even friends destroy each other, but there is a Friend who loves more faithfully than a brother."[32]

Are you the type of friend you would want to have? Why or why not?

Jesus had a very tight-knit group of twelve disciples, but His circle of core friends included only three — Peter, James, and John.

Read John 15:15. What did Jesus call His close companions?

Can a family member be a friend? Why or why not?

Sometimes we may not keep a friend's prayer request private. How can this feel like betrayal?

Edification

Read Proverbs 27:17, then summarize what it says.

Rubbing two blades together makes each knife sharper, more effective, and more useful. What are some practical ways friends sharpen each other?

In what ways has a friend made you better?

In what ways are you making a friend better?

When have a friend's words hurt you?

Which is more hurtful, words from someone you don't necessarily care about or words from a friend?

Notes

Reciprocation

There may be seasons in a friendship where one person is not able to give as much as the other, but generally speaking, in successful friendships both persons are equal participants in the relationship. They each give and take of their time and resources.

In his commentary titled *Exposition of the Bible* John Gill's writes:

> Friendship ought to be mutual and reciprocal, as between David and Jonathan; a man that receives friendship ought to return it, or otherwise he is guilty of great ingratitude.[33]

Not all friendships will last forever. Some come about for spiritual growth; others come along during adversity and pain, at a time when God knows we need them. Some friendships dissipate because of major life changes: marriage or divorce, children, job opportunities or job disappointments, relocation, or death.

Regardless of their length, treasure your friendships as a gift from God. If the friendship left scars, be thankful for the lessons learned.

In the table below, read the verses listed on the left and summarize them on the right.

Proverbs 3:3	
Proverbs 17:17	
Ecclesiastes 4:9–10	
Matthew 7:12	
John 13:34	
Romans 12:15	
Galatians 6:2	
Ephesians 4:32	
1 Thessalonians 5:11	

From these verses what can you conclude about friendships?

Notes

If you are seeking friendship, ask God to help you identify what you need and to send you that special friend.

Ultimately, Jesus is our best friend. He is loyal and faithful and will stick closer than any other. But in His goodness, He provides earthly friends too. And when you sidle up to your closest relationships and exchange some Winnie-the-Pooh-type encouragement, you will sparkle.

What Meant the Most to You from Today's Study?

Application

- Make (or buy) a card for your friend. Then write, "25 Great Things About You."

- Listen to "Friends Are Friends Forever" By Michael W. Smith: https://www.youtube.com/watch?v=Ped1jYLFtkA

Notes

Light from the Scriptures

Teach me, O Lord, the way of Your statutes, And I shall observe it to the end.

Give me understanding, that I may observe Your law and keep it with all my heart. Make me walk in the path of Your commandments, for I delight in it. Incline my heart to Your testimonies and not to dishonest gain. Turn away my eyes from looking at vanity, and revive me in Your ways. Establish Your word to Your servant, as that which produces reverence for You. Turn away my reproach which I dread, for Your ordinances are good. Behold, I long for Your precepts; Revive me through Your righteousness.

Psalm 119:33–40

> Core friends have our best interests in mind. They lift us up, affirm our dreams and passions, encourage us to persevere, and generally inspire us. We laugh and cry with these friends. These friends want to see us shine!

❧ 12 ☙
When Things Don't Make Sense

Focus: We shine when we trust God.

Real satisfaction comes not in understanding God's motives, but in understanding His character, in trusting in His promises, and in leaning on Him and resting in Him as the Sovereign who knows what He is doing and does all things well.

~ Joni Eareckson Tada

My husband asked seventeen-year-old Will to call the dog in for the night. Will pressed the button to raise the electric garage door and began whistling and calling, "Buddy, Buddy, come on Buddy." Although it was a dark, moonless night, the dim garage light enabled Will to see Buddy pacing back and forth out on the driveway and barking loudly. Will couldn't understand why Buddy continued pacing and wouldn't come in. He whistled and called Buddy's name for 3–4 more minutes.

Realizing something was wrong, Will called to his dad, "I need your help. I don't know why Buddy won't come inside. He keeps pacing back and forth in front of the garage."

After getting a good look, my husband's expression turned from quizzical to shocked.

"I'll tell ya why," he said. "That's not Buddy . . . *that's a bear!*"

Buddy was around the corner of the house barking at the bear. Maybe he was trying to alert Will . . . or perhaps he was trying to distract Will so he wouldn't move any further into the bear's territory.

Shock finally gave way to laughter; bear sightings are a normal occurrence in our neighborhood. We got Buddy in through another door, and everything turned out fine.

Notes

Things weren't what they seemed. Will heard Buddy barking and thought he was looking at his dog, not a bear. Trying to persuade a bear to come into the garage wasn't Will's intent either. What he thought was right would've been very wrong.

Sometimes our sight can fail, and limited perception can misguide. Trusting what we think is right may give us an unwelcome surprise.

Reflect on a time when something wasn't as it seemed. What did you do? What was the outcome?

Has God ever led you to take action but the obstacles seemed too great? If so, write about it.

The obstacles seemed massive in the following passage of Scripture. Read Numbers 13:1–33. Who spoke to Moses and what did he direct him to do? (vv. 1–2)

This wasn't hearsay or gossip running throughout the camp. This direction was given by almighty God.

The spies are identified in verses 4–16. Two of the spies were Joshua and Caleb. How long did they spy? (vv. 21–25)

What did they discover? (v. 27)

How did they describe the people? (v. 28)

What did Caleb say they must do? (v. 30)

How did the other men who had gone up with Caleb and Joshua describe the land? (vv. 31–33)

Ten of the spies saw the magnitude of their problem. They saw with human eyes the impossibilities and enormous obstacles — literally. The people were considered "giants," due to their height. Joshua and Caleb, however, saw things from a different perspective. They trusted in what they couldn't see — the power of God to overtake the enemy and accomplish what He said would be done.

Read Numbers 14:6–9. In verse nine what did Caleb and Joshua say to the people?

Only do not rebel against the LORD; and do not fear the people of the land, for they will be our prey. Their protection has been removed from them, and the LORD is _____; do not _____."

What question did the Lord ask Moses? (v. 11)

How would you respond if God asked this question of you?

105

Notes

Joshua and Caleb trusted and obeyed God's commands. Their faith enabled them to move with full confidence and claim victory, even though it appeared to be an impossible challenge. By remembering God's prior provision, they were provided with fresh strength and courage.

When, if ever, has God called you to a particular task, but you thought others seemed better suited for the work? Explain.

Perhaps, you're moving forward despite your circumstances. What obstacles do you face? Who or what, are your giants?

What doesn't make sense?

What would take a miracle?

Looking back at how God has been faithful to you in the past will enable you to trust Him in the present.

In the Bible, the word trust means a bold, confident, sure security or an action based on that security.[34]

What makes you decide to trust someone? Is trust earned? Is it proven?

What makes you decide to trust in something?

What destroys your trust?

Notes

Anyone and anything can destroy our trust. And although we strive to be trustworthy ourselves, we're human, born with a sin nature and prone to be untrustworthy as well.

There is only One who is completely trustworthy.

Numbers 23:19 tells us this: *God is not a man, that He should lie, nor a son of man, that He should repent; Has He said, and will He not do it? Or has He spoken, and will He not make it good?*

God is worthy of our trust because:

- His love is without deception and never-ending. In Psalm 86:15 we read: *But you, O Lord, are a God merciful and gracious, slow to anger and abounding in steadfast love and faithfulness* (ESV).

- His Word tells us He is reliable. Psalm 111:7 says *the works of His hands are faithful and just; all His precepts are trustworthy* (NIV).

- Trustworthiness is in God's nature. Deuteronomy 7:9 tells us: *Know therefore that the LORD your God, He is God, the faithful God, who keeps His covenant and His lovingkindness to a thousandth generation with those who love Him and keep His commandments.*

- His power can make the impossible, possible. Jeremiah 10:12 tells us *it is He who made the earth by His power, Who established the world by His wisdom; And by His understanding He has stretched out the heavens.*

What would confidence in God look like for you right now? On the next page, fill in the blanks. For example, trusting in God would mean *less worry, more peace.*

Less _____, more _____

Less _____, more _____

Less _____, more _____

Less _____, more _____

Notes

If this is a struggle, admit it to God; He already knows your thoughts and fears. Pray something like this:

> God I want to trust You. I know You have everything under control, and You do only what is for my good. When I'm confused, help me trust You. When I don't know what to do, help me trust You. When I'm disappointed, help me trust You. When I'm frightened with what the future holds, help me trust You. In everything, help me trust You. Amen.

We have God's Word that we can trust in what we cannot see. Proverbs 3:5–6 tells us, *Trust in the Lord with all your heart and do not lean on your own understanding. In all your ways acknowledge Him, and He will make your paths straight.*

We may not be able to see in the dark, but God can — and we can trust Him.

What Meant the Most to You from Today's Study?

Application

- Read Jim Cymbala's book *Fresh Faith*.
- Listen to "Trust in You" by Laura Daigle. https://www.youtube.com/watch?v=n_aVFVveJNs.

Light from the Scriptures

Submit therefore to God. Resist the devil and he will flee from you. Draw near to God and He will draw near to you. Cleanse your hands, you sinners; and purify your hearts, you double-minded. Be miserable and mourn and weep; let your laughter be turned into mourning and your joy to gloom. Humble yourselves in the presence of the Lord, and He will exalt you. Do not speak against one another, brethren. He who speaks against a brother or judges his brother, speaks against the law and judges the law; but if you judge the law, you are not a doer of the law but a judge of it. There is only one Lawgiver and Judge, the One who is able to save and to destroy; but who are you who judge your neighbor? Come now, you who say, "Today or tomorrow we will go to such and such a city, and spend a year there and engage in business and make a profit." Yet you do not know what your life will be like tomorrow. You are just a vapor that appears for a little while and then vanishes away. Instead, you ought to say, "If the Lord wills, we will live and also do this or that." But as it is, you boast in your arrogance; all such boasting is evil. Therefore, to one who knows the right thing to do and does not do it, to him it is sin.

James 4:7–17

> Sometimes our insight can fail, and limited perception can misguide. Trusting what we think is right may surprise us.

❦ 13 ❧
Hate: How We Hide, Deny, and Justify

Focus: We shine when we seek God's help when struggling with strong emotions.

You can be sure you are abiding in Christ if you are able to have a Christlike love toward the people that irritate you the most.

~ Vonette Bright
Author, speaker, Co-founder of Campus Crusade for Christ

> IT WAS A SCORCHING HOT JUNE DAY. OR MAYBE IT FELT HOTTER to me because I was pregnant — only six weeks away from delivering my son. I had just finished teaching an afternoon class and was looking forward to sitting on the covered front porch's swing and sipping a cold glass of lemonade.
> But when I returned home, a flurry of people and several cars crowded my driveway.
> "Your dad's been in an accident," Alan said.
> "Then we should go to the hospital," I quickly replied.
> The look in his eyes and his silence spoke volumes. He began to cry and then I knew that my father was dead. I moaned loudly while my husband held me.
> "How?" I managed to ask.
> "Robbery attempt. He was shot through the heart and killed instantly."
> I continued to sob. My unborn son would never meet his grandfather. I felt emotions I'd never felt before. I hated these men who murdered my father.

We hide, deny, or justify. Suppressing hate or other undesirable emotions in the deep places of our heart can protect the image we strive to project. We might conceal our emotions because we innately know something is wrong, or maybe we choose denial and pretend that such emotions don't exist. For many, justification is easiest: *After all, if you knew what he/she did, you'd understand.*

Hate is real.

Maybe you want to skip this chapter because it doesn't apply to you — except that hate is often accompanied by anger and the inability to forgive.

Which of the following statements can you identify with most?

- I would never hate anyone. I go to church and read my Bible. After all, I'm a Christian and real Christians don't hate.
- Okay. Maybe I don't "like," but I definitely don't hate.
- Love? Forgive? Oh no way . . . you have no idea what he/she did to me.
- Hmm. Maybe I do have hate and anger I've never dealt with.
- I feel like I should hate but I don't. I feel sadness. I feel sorry for him/her.
- Other _____.

Hate can be defined as "intense hostility and aversion usually derived from fear, anger, or sense of injury; extreme dislike or disgust."[35]

Read Titus 3:3. Paul was writing to encourage Titus. How did Paul describe his foolish behaviors before coming to Christ?

Paul remarked that his hate and other disobedient sins were foolish.

My father's funeral concluded and weeks passed. Life fell back into its normal routines — except there was nothing normal about what I was feeling. I suppressed my hate but continued my morning routine — an early 5:30 A.M. devotion and prayer time with God. John 14:15 flew off the page. *"If you love Me, you will keep My commandments."*

With genuine affection I responded, *I love you, God*! Even as I said it, I stammered. The emotion surprised me as I looked around the room to see if God was looking. Weird, right?

Notes

Something was wrong and I knew what it was. First John 4:7 tells us to love one another. I was being disobedient. Tears spilled from my eyes and left wet splotches on my open Bible.

I don't hate anyone — I strongly dislike them! I protested. I continued my justifying rant. *They deserve to be hated for the crimes they have committed.*

But in the stillness and quiet of the morning, God changed my heart. My love for God moved me to sorrow. I admitted what I had been hiding and began to understand that loving God meant obeying Him. And this meant loving all people.

Confessing my sin was a relief — and the easy part. Now I wondered how I could dump my wrong attitude.

Dozens of reality TV stars boast about hating another person. What is the difference between Paul's confession and transformation and the person who boasts about hating people? What is the difference between short-term hate — like toward a driver who cuts you off — and long-term, deep hate?

From the world's perspective, conquering hate, or any other wrong emotion, appears nearly impossible. Read 1 John 4:4. The context of this verse is identifying false teachers. John reminds the reader of the power they have in Christ. The same power that exposes false teachers can also enable us to resist the urge to continue hating. Who does John say is greater than any of our troubles?

Now Read Luke 10:19 and 2 Corinthians 12:10. What is the common theme in these verses along with 1 John 4:4?

When we succumb to wrong attitudes, what does God provide?

Notes

John reminds us there is power for the believer to overcome all sin, including the sin of hate.

Read Isaiah 41:10. What three things does God say He will do?

Second Peter 1:3–4 (NLT) tells us *by his divine power, God has given us everything we need for living a godly life. We have received all of this by coming to know him, the one who called us to himself by means of his marvelous glory and excellence. And because of his glory and excellence, he has given us great and precious promises. These are the promises that enable you to share his divine nature and escape the world's corruption caused by human desires.*

Wow! Don't miss this. Underline the first sentence. God has given us everything we need to escape the world's corruption — which includes hate — and has made it possible to live a godly life.

How do these verses encourage you?

Based on what we've covered, have you ever felt hate or anger toward someone? If yes, have you dealt with it? Were you — or are you — a hider, a denier, or justifier? If no, is there another emotion that holds you captive?

God has enabled each of us to identify our emotions, and He empowers us to deal with them appropriately.

Maybe you've experienced:
- Betrayal of a spouse
- Betrayal of a best friend
- Devastating gossip
- A backstabbing co-worker
- Jealousy that led to hate
- A life taken too soon
- Evil that prevailed over justice
- A boss who fired you without cause

God doesn't overlook the evil done. He sees your pain. God also knows hate, anger, and the inability to forgive are toxic emotions. They affect us in two ways.

1. Our health
2. Our relationship with God

Our Health

Cardiologist Dr. Cynthia Thaik revealed the dangers of short-and long-term health problems that have been linked to unmanaged anger.[36] They include:
- headaches
- heart disease
- immune problems
- digestion problems, such as abdominal pain
- insomnia
- increased anxiety
- depression
- high blood pressure
- skin problems, such as eczema
- heart attack
- stroke

For the sake of our physical health, we must diffuse hate, anger, and the unforgiveness that often accompanies theses emotions. What steps will you take to overcome these powerful emotions?

Forgiveness doesn't negate consequences. Neither does it require a restored relationship. It means releasing unforgiveness to God and allowing Him to be our refuge and the executer of perfect, righteous judgment.

Our Relationship with God

Refusing to deal with hate and anger changes our relationship with God.

Read Psalm 66:18. If I have _____ _____ God will not _____.

But here is great news. Read 1 John 1:9. If we do what, God will do what?

Read 1 Corinthians 13:4–7 written here: *Love is patient and kind; love does not envy or boast; it is not arrogant or rude. It does not insist on its own way; it is not irritable or resentful; it does not rejoice at wrongdoing, but rejoices with the truth. Love bears all things, believes all things, hopes all things, endures all things.* (ESV)

Circle the words in the verses that describe Christ-like love.

Love is the opposite of hate. To love people means we don't wish them any harm. We aren't happy to hear of their pain or misfortune, and we don't behave in a way that is rude in front of them.

I had already admitted what I was hiding. I wondered if God expected me to love hateful people the way I love my best friends. For the next two days, I prayed constantly and searched the Scriptures for answers. *What do I do now, God? I don't want to disobey You by not loving. I can't do this on my own. Please change my heart.* My hate was still there and I was worried.

Within twenty-four hours of earnestly praying, God gave me the answer. While having lunch with a friend, I opened my Bible to read a verse that I thought would answer a question she had just asked. I turned to Ephesians 6:12 and began reading. Before I

Notes

finished reading, I began to sob. I knew I had received my answer. I felt free. Healed.

Read Ephesians 6:12 written here:

> *Our struggle is not against flesh and blood, but against the rulers, against the powers, against the world forces of this darkness, against the spiritual forces of wickedness in the heavenly places.*

Based on this verse, who is the real enemy?

Our fight isn't with another person. Our fight is with Satan, and we can transfer our hate to him, where it belongs.

Is there ever a time to hate? If so, whom or what do we hate?

After God opened my eyes, my hateful thoughts became less frequent. And over time, the hate dissolved completely. There is no evidence that God changed the murderers' hearts. But that year God changed me.

You can be free too.
- Be transparent with God. Tell Him the truth.
- Identify who is at the forefront of your battle.
- Pray frequently, especially when the person you hate comes to mind. Ask God for strength.
- Ask God to forgive you.
- Pray for the person you hate.
- Read the Bible for wisdom, strength, and direction.

First John 2:9–10 tells us *the one who says he is in the Light and yet hates his brother is in the darkness until now. The one who loves his brother abides in the Light and there is no cause for stumbling in him.*

Today we choose. Let's refuse to let hate tarnish our radiant light.

What Meant the Most to You from Today's Study?

Application

- Write Ephesians 6:12 on a sticky note and place it on your mirror. Refer to it as often as necessary to remind you that Satan is the real enemy when people make you angry, or treat you in a way that would invoke a hateful response,

- Read Carol Kent's book *When I Lay My Isaac Down*.

- Listen to "Forgiveness" by Matthew West. https://www.youtube.com/watch?v=h1Lu5udXEZI

Light from the Scriptures

Put on then, as God's chosen ones, holy and beloved, compassionate hearts, kindness, humility, meekness, and patience, bearing with one another and, if one has a complaint against another, forgiving each other; as the Lord has forgiven you, so you also must forgive. And above all these put on love, which binds everything together in perfect harmony. And let the peace of Christ rule in your hearts, to which indeed you were called in one body. And be thankful. Let the word of Christ dwell in you richly, teaching and admonishing one another in all wisdom, singing psalms and hymns and spiritual songs, with thankfulness in your hearts to God. And whatever you do, in word or deed, do everything in the name of the Lord Jesus, giving thanks to God the Father through him.

Colossians 3:12–17 ESV

Notes

After God opened my eyes, my hateful thoughts became less frequent. And over time, the hate dissolved completely. There is no evidence that God changed the murderer's heart. But that year God changed me.

❧ 14 ❧
Unleash the Power

Focus:
We shine when we utilize the power within us.

Through my prayers I can change the destiny of a life.
I don't move a muscle, but I help move the hand of God.

~ Joni Eareckson Tada

> "WOMAN IN RAGS, GARBAGE REVEALED AS HEIRESS," READ THE headline in the *San Francisco Chronicle* concerning a lady, known as "Garbage Mary" who was picked up in a shopping mall in Delray Beach, Florida. She appeared to be just another derelict whose mind had faded. Neighbors told stories of her scrounging through garbage cans for food, which she hoarded in her car and her two-bedroom apartment. There were mounds of garbage in the small apartment, stuffed in the refrigerator, the stove, the sink, the cabinets, and the bathtub. There were paths between the garbage. Other than in the kitchen, there was nowhere to sit because everything was piled high with trash. Police finally identified Mary as the daughter of a well-to-do lawyer and bank director from Illinois who had died several years earlier. In addition to the garbage, the police found Mobil Oil stock worth more than four hundred thousand dollars; documents indicating ownership of oil fields in Kansas; stock certificates from firms such as US Steel, Uniroyal, and Squibb; and passbooks for eight large bank accounts. Garbage Mary was a millionaire living as a derelict. Untold wealth was at her disposal, yet she scrounged through garbage rather than claim the resources that were rightly hers by inheritance."[37]

For whatever reason, Mary didn't know or didn't care that she had so much at her fingertips. In what ways do we have the potential to be like Mary?

How do we sometimes choose to live like spiritual paupers?

Notes

One year, during a CMA's *Country Christmas* on ABC, Tony Award-winning singer and actress Idina Menzel was asked what made the movie *Frozen* different. She replied, "It's about unleashing the power within." We can't know the power she is referring to, but as Christ-followers, we have access to the mightiest and strongest power source of all.

Dictionaries offer many definitions of *power* including "the ability to act or produce an effect."[38] When we pray to our mighty Father, our prayers change circumstances, outcomes, minds, hearts, and people. Our prayers produce an effect.

Read Nehemiah chapter 1. Nehemiah had received bad news from Jerusalem.

Nehemiah 1:4 sheds light on his emotional state: Nehemiah wept and mourned for days. What are two other things he did?

Nehemiah's prayer is recorded in Nehemiah 1:5–6. What do you deduce about his faith in God?

In God's providence, Nehemiah was positioned and equipped to approach the king, which he courageously did. He asked for resources to rebuild the wall in Jerusalem and restore the people. He successfully accomplished the task in fifty-two days.

Nehemiah was a great leader because he had faith and a plan. Before he acted, he:

- Prayed
- Fasted
- Confessed sin
- Praised God

Notes

If we're honest with ourselves, can we say that prayer is the first thing we do when confronting our battles? Or do we call a friend first? When we fight our battles on our knees as Nehemiah did, we win every time. The outcome may look different than we envisioned, but when God's power is unleashed there's a plan and a purpose.

Yes, God is powerful. When we're communicating with God through prayer, Satan knows he's about to be stripped of all his power, so he cleverly uses a variety of tools and methods to ensure we don't do what we intended to do — pray.

How satisfied are you with your prayer life?

What, if anything, keeps you from spending time in prayer? Circle any that apply.

    Busyness   Distractions   Unbelief

    Guilt   Other priorities   Other_____

The answer may appear obvious at first glance, but for the sake of seeing it in writing, how does busyness keep us from praying?

Busyness is seemingly innocent; yet it is a powerful tool the devil uses to keep us from praying. Consider your own schedule. How do you balance work, family, and friends?

If prayer is as important as work and family, then we need to deliberately plan for it. Sounds strange maybe — scheduling prayer. We'll come back to scheduling prayer, but first let's think about other reasons we put off or avoid prayer.

In what way does guilt prevent us from praying?

What about unbelief?

Do you sometimes think God is unwilling to answer prayers? Why or why not?

If you answered yes, why would He be unwilling?

Maintaining a prayer life is life changing. Understanding the why, when, and how of prayer are critical and necessary steps. The following are guidelines to help us get started:

1. Pray naturally.

Prayer is the bridge that connects us to God, creating a deeper relationship with Him. Your relationship with God is as unique as you are, and your prayers will reflect what you believe about Him. Use words you're most comfortable with and express what's on your heart. A large, sophisticated vocabulary is not necessary. Sometimes we can tell God our needs with tears or sighs. Pray as sincerely and honestly as you know how. Tell God everything. His mercy, grace, love, and forgiveness are limitless.

Are you comfortable articulating your thoughts to God? Why or why not?

Notes

If you're not comfortable, what's holding you back?

Language doesn't determine whether a prayer is wimpy or powerful. It's the attitude and confidence behind the words, and the belief in the One to whom we're praying that determines a prayer's effectiveness. Rambling rhetoric is useless when the person speaking doubts God's power or interest. Conversely, "help me" uttered from sincere humility causes God to incline His ear.

2. Grasp who God is.

Prayer isn't a conversation with another person who is powerless. Prayer is communication with God — the Creator of the universe! To help us fully understand the depth of this, read Isaiah 6:1–3.

Where is the Lord sitting?

What is He wearing?

What are the seraphim saying?

In the Hebrew language, any word that is repeated consecutively three times is important. To repeat the word *holy* three times states completion or absoluteness. "Holy, holy, holy" is only used twice in the Bible — once in Isaiah and again in Revelation.[39]

Now read Philippians 2:10–11. What is the response of every single person?

If you struggle with believing that God is holy and powerful, ask God to help you believe.

Read Matthew 8:23–27. What did Jesus do? Based on this text, what is Jesus capable of doing?

How will this change how you approach God in prayer?

Read Jeremiah 32:17, 27. What is too hard for God?

What hard prayer do you need answered?

3. Pray often.

In Luke 18:1–8 Jesus directed His disciples to pray. In 1 Peter 4:7 Peter said to be self-controlled and pray. James 5:16 tells us to pray for each other.

Read 1 Thessalonians 5:17. Circle what Paul says the frequency of our prayers should be:

   Daily   Weekly   As needed   Continuous

Are you the kind of person who prays about something once and then trusts God to handle it, or are you the type who prays often for the same thing?

First Samuel 12:23 tells us that neglecting to pray is _____ .

Notes

How often do we boldly state our profession of faith in God, yet, based on our time spent in prayer, we act as if He is nonexistent? Be honest with yourself and God. When do you most often run to God in prayer?

Conversely, is there a time or season of life that you forget to pray?

For those comfortable talking with God, the natural process enables them to commune while driving, cooking, or waiting in line at the grocery store. There's nothing wrong with praying during these times. Prayer is effective regardless of the time and place. Consider the distractions, however, of watching the traffic light and measuring ingredients.

What distracts you?

To eliminate distractions, we can plan for deliberate, intentional, closed-eyes time for prayer. We can get up early or stay up late. Where is your special place and time to have quiet, uninterrupted prayer?

4. Ask God to forgive your sins.

Read Psalm 66:18. According to this verse, what hinders communication with God?

We're created for relationship with God. He lovingly convicts us of sin because He wants nothing standing in the way of our relationship with Him. Satan's destructive scheme is to separate us from God. He condemns us with his lies in hopes that we'll be ashamed and hide from God. He whispers we're busy and our time with God can wait, or that our sin has made us too guilty to approach God. God's conviction isn't intended to push us away; it's meant to turn us around and draw us back to Him. That's how much He loves us.

Take a moment now and ask God to reveal any sin that would hamper your relationship with Him. What do you think He's showing you?

Communication with God also involves listening. Be focused and allow God to speak to your spirit as you read His Word. Reflect on how God has been faithful in the past. This will be your hope for the future. Make connections. This is God speaking to you.

5. Pray like you believe His Word.

Recall Hebrews 4:16. God invites us to approach His throne. Summarize this verse.

With confidence, call out to God. We don't have to convince Him of our brokenness, desperate state, or the severity of our troubles. He knows. God loves us and desires to help. He is filled with compassion and mercy.

Read Ephesians 3:20 and fill in the missing word(s).

God is able to do _____
more than we ask.

Read Philippians 4:6–7. With thanksgiving, we're free to tell God everything — including every anxious thought. What anxious thoughts are you fighting today?

Notes

Synonyms for anxious include *worry, fear, nervous, concerned, uneasy, apprehensive,* and *restless*. (Note that *anxious* does not mean eager.) Do any of these apply to you?

God knows everything. Why do you think we're instructed to tell God what we need?

Why do you think we're told to make those requests with thanksgiving?

In Psalm 119:18 we read these words: ***Open my eyes, that I may behold wonderful things from Your law.*** What do you think it means to ask God to open our eyes?

Refer to the quote by Joni Eareckson Tada at the beginning of this chapter. In your own words, write what you think she means.

How will you apply her thoughts to your situation today?

Let's unleash the power of God. We'll do as Philippians 2:15 says and ***shine among the people like stars in the sky*** (NIV).

What Meant the Most to You from Today's Study?   *Notes*

Application

- Start a prayer group with friends, new people from church, or neighbors. Commit to the priority of praying — the reason you've gathered. Socializing can become a distraction. Decide with your group on a day to meet, either weekly or bi-weekly. Stick to the schedule as much as possible.

- If you like to write, purchase a journal to write out your prayers. If you like to draw, doodle your prayers.

- Read Beth Moore's book *Praying God's Word*.

- Listen to "Lord, I Need You" by Matt Maher https://www.youtube.com/watch?v=LuvfMDhTyMA

- Research done on habits reveals that it takes twenty-one days to start or stop a habit. Commit to pray for twenty-one days about one important area, situation, or relationship in your life.

> *If prayer is as important as work and family, then we need to deliberately plan for it.*

Light from the Scriptures

I thank my God every time I remember you. In all my prayers for all of you, I always pray with joy because of your partnership in the gospel from the first day until now, being confident of this, that he who began a good work in you will carry it on to completion until the day of Christ Jesus. It is right for me to feel this way about all of you, since I have you in my heart and, whether I am in chains or defending and confirming the gospel, all of you share in God's grace with me. God can testify how I long for all of you with the affection of Christ Jesus. And this is my prayer: that your love may abound more and more in knowledge and depth of insight, so that you may be able to discern what is best and may be pure and blameless for the day of Christ, filled with the fruit of righteousness that comes through Jesus Christ–to the glory and praise of God.

Philippians 1:3–13 NIV

15

Another Day, Another Decision

Focus: We shine when we trust God to help us make the right decisions.

God doesn't want people to do what they think is best: He wants them to do what He knows is best, and no amount of reasoning and intellectualizing will discover that.

~ Henry T. Blackaby
Preacher and Author, *Experiencing God*

SEVERAL YEARS AGO, I WAS INVITED TO SPEAK AT AN EDUCATION conference. I looked forward to my time alone at the conference to get some clarity about family decisions that needed to be made. In preparation for my weekend trip, I had prayed for thirty days asking God to reveal His truth to me.

When the time arrived, my accommodations were in a cozy hotel room located on the twenty-eighth floor. After settling in, I opened the Bible. Expecting God to meet me there, I read and prayed. Three hours passed. Nothing. Quiet. I was looking for an epiphany, but the hours spent with God were ordinary — like my time at home — and left me feeling disappointed.

I closed my Bible, pulled up a comfy chair, and peered out the picture window that framed a breathtaking sunset. From that height, I could see for miles. My gaze was drawn to a traffic jam on the interstate. Traffic was gridlocked; cars were backed up for miles. Sirens blared as emergency vehicles sped by. Instead of a peaceful view, I saw a disaster on the highway.

As cars approached the on ramp I whispered, "You'd better slow down. You don't know what's coming." From my bird's-eye view I could see both impending dangers and the better route.

"If you knew what lies ahead, you'd go the other way," I continued. "Hold up! There's a wreck ahead and you're about to wind up in it." I pushed up from my chair, shook my index finger at the traffic and vehemently chastised, "If you knew what I know, you'd go the other way!"

Unexpectedly, God whispered to my heart. *"That's just like Me. I know what's on your path. I see impending danger, and I put up roadblocks to prevent mistakes. You can trust Me to help you make the right decision and put you on the best road."*

I drew in a long breath and exhaled slowly. The scene outside my window was an answer to my prayer. I have limited perspective, but God can see the future.

Making decisions is a daily responsibility for all of us — everything from selecting childcare to choosing a career. Often, these decisions confuse or overwhelm us. We're either stuck in traffic with no ability to move forward, or we're at a fork in the road and don't know which way to go.

As king of Judah, Jehoshaphat, the son of Asa and a descendent of King David, had the momentous responsibility of making decisions for all of Judea. One specific example is recorded in 2 Chronicles 20:1–25. Jehoshaphat needed to make decisions about an impending battle. Read this passage in its entirety to get a complete picture of what was happening.

Jehoshaphat was a good king and a great leader. Verse three explains his success. Whom did Jehoshaphat seek when he was afraid?

Below, circle all that Jehoshaphat did (vv. 2–4).

Proclaimed a fast   Went fishing   Admitted dependence

Inquired of the Lord   Slept for three days   Sought the Lord

Instructed the people to seek God's help

Circle which action best describes Jehoshaphat's attitude toward God.

   Resistant   Dependent   Mocking

How did Jehoshaphat praise God? What was his prayer based on? (vv. 5–9)

Read 2 Chronicles 20:12 written here and fill in the missing words:
O our God, will You not judge them? For we are powerless before this great multitude who are coming against us; _____ but our eyes are on You.

Notes

Notes

Our prayers of complete dependence on God bring Him glory! We can verbalize, "I don't know what to do, but I'll keep my eyes on you, God."

How is seeking God (v. 3) and putting our eyes on Him (v. 12) the same thing?

Identify three ways God responded to Jehoshaphat's requests and, consequently, rewarded his acts of obedience (vv. 15–17).

Finally, identify four ways Jehoshaphat reacted to God's words (vv. 18–21).

The end result was _____ _____ (v. 22).

Victory is the result of seeking God.

First Chronicles 22:19 tells us, *Now set your mind and heart to seek the Lord your God.* John Piper writes that seeking God "is the conscious fixing or focusing of our mind's attention and our heart's affection on God."[40]

That sums up Jehoshaphat:

- He sought God and kept his eyes on Him.
- He praised God for His attributes.
- He bowed his head low to the ground (indicating he was on his knees or prostrate).
- He was an example to the people he led.
- He remembered God's prior faithfulness.

We can follow Jehoshaphat's example when making decisions. We look to our faithful God and ask for His guidance. The Scriptures provide powerful prayers. Just pray this way, for example:

You said, *Your ears will hear a word behind you, "This is the way, walk in it," whenever you turn to the right or to the left.* Isaiah 30:21

You said, *I will instruct you and teach you in the way you should go; I will counsel you with my loving eye on you.* Psalm 32:8 NIV

You said, *Call to me, and I will answer you, and show you great and mighty things, you do not know.* Jeremiah 33:3 NKJV

You said, *I will make all My mountains a road, And My highways will be raised up.* Isaiah 49:11

You said, *Show me Your ways, LORD, teach me Your paths. Guide me in Your truth and teach me, for You are God my Savior, and my hope is in You all day long.* Psalm 25:4–5

Additionally, Jehoshaphat proclaimed a fast. The idea is to "give up something" to focus on something else. As described in Scripture, to fast is to abstain from food and/or drink for religious devotion. Fasting is not commanded in the Bible, but there's evidence of fasting in both the Old and New Testaments. Author Eugene H. Merrill tells us this:

> Fasting appears to be a private matter in the Bible, an expression of personal devotion linked to three major kinds of crisis in life: lamentation/penitence, mourning, and petition. Without exception, it has to do with a sense of need and dependence, of abject helplessness in the face of actual or anticipated calamity. It is in examining these situations that the theological meaning and value of fasting are to be discovered.[41]

Jehoshaphat admitted dependence. You, also, are making important decisions, perhaps life-changing ones. There is never a time to function independently from God. Admit you want and need God's help.

While I was at the hotel, I observed drivers making decisions based on what they thought was the best way to go. They couldn't have known the road would lead to a wreck. But from high above,

Notes

I saw what was down the road. God wants to lead us away from a potential wreck of wrong choices. Since we can't see the future the way God does, it's imperative we continue in prayer and Bible study and trust that God will lead us in the right direction.

Recall Proverbs 3:5–6 written here: *Trust in the Lord with all your heart and lean not on your own understanding; in all your ways submit to Him, and He will make your paths straight* (NIV).

Circle "lean not on your own understanding." Put a box around "submit to him, and He will make your paths straight."

What parts are our responsibility? Which part is God's?

That evening at the hotel, the sun sank into the horizon and the sky darkened, but my heart was light with the peace that passes all understanding. I knew God was steering me to the right path.

God knows what's around your next corner and what lies ahead as you travel your road. We may not understand why God erects certain road blocks, but we can put our faith in Him. Let's stay focused on the sunsets and not the traffic jams in life.

Psalm 119:105 reminds us this: *Your word is a lamp to my feet and a light to my path. When we allow God to light our path, we'll shine like a beaming light.*

What Meant the Most to You from Today's Study?

Application

- Create a personal action plan following the example that Jehoshaphat set:

My Personal Plan

Today I am seeking God for clarity on this decision:

I praise God for:

The place and time I plan to consistently pray is:

The scripture I will focus on today to pray back to God is:

One thing that God has done for me in the past is:

To make extra time, I will give up:

- Listen to "God Is in Control" by Twila Paris. https://www.youtube.com/watch?v=r6Eiv1r5UnE

> ⚜
> God knows what's around your corner and what lies at the end of your road. We may not understand why God erects certain road blocks, but we can put our faith in Him.
> ⚜

Light from the Scriptures

For this reason I bow my knees before the Father, from whom every family in heaven and on earth derives its name, that He would grant you, according to the riches of His glory, to be strengthened with power through His Spirit in the inner man, so that Christ may dwell in your hearts through faith; and that you, being rooted and grounded in love, may be able to comprehend with all the saints what is the breadth and length and height and depth, and to know the love of Christ which surpasses knowledge, that you may be filled up to all the fullness of God. Now to Him who is able to do far more abundantly beyond all that we ask or think, according to the power that works within us, to Him be the glory in the church and in Christ Jesus to all generations forever and ever. Amen.

Ephesians 3:14–20

Notes

Focus: We shine when we're real with ourselves and with God.

❧ 16 ☙
What's Hidden in Our Pockets?

There is nothing hidden from the Lord's eyes. There are no secrets with Him. Alone or in company, by night or by day, in private or public, He is acquainted with all our ways.

~ J. C. Ryle
Nineteenth-Century Evangelical Preacher and Author

IN FIRST GRADE, WILL BECAME INTERESTED IN TRADING CARDS. To make sure he didn't take cards or other toys to school (per the school's policy), I habitually checked his backpack for stowaways of any kind. One particular morning, he passed the card and toy test, and I drove him to school.

When I picked him up from school, I was shocked to see him showing his cards to a teacher.

"Will," I said, "I checked your backpack and you didn't have those. Where did you get them?"

He responded, "They were in my pocket."

The next morning, this mother was all the wiser. I checked Will's backpack, his coat pockets, and his pants pockets. "Good. You're ready for school," I said. You can imagine my complete shock when I picked him up from school and he was showing his cards to yet another teacher!

Frustrated I said, "Will, you didn't have those cards this morning. I checked your backpack, your coat pockets, and your pants pockets." Eyes downcast, he mumbled, "You didn't check my underwear."

Envision the subsequent morning!

In the hours that followed, I thought about my son's deception and how sometimes children hide things from their parents. Then unexpectedly, by the leading of the Holy Spirit, a thought came to my mind. *Is there anything you're hiding from Me?*

Hiding things can be innocent. Do you recall the childhood game, Hide and Seek? The rules were simple. You needed two or more players. One person covered his eyes while the others hid. Then the person whose eyes had been covered tried to find those who were hidden. We didn't have to travel far to hide — we hid in the backyard. The swing set and trees easily concealed our whereabouts.

Today we don't need multiple players to play this game. Our culture has allowed us to master "hiding" alone. How? We hide what we don't want people to know.

The dictionary defines *hide* this way:

1. To put out of sight; to conceal for shelter or protection.
2. To keep secret; hide the truth.
3. To turn (the eyes or face) away in shame or anger.[42]

Usually childhood antics or games are harmless, as the first definition suggests. But hiding something from God is a more serious matter.

What kinds of things do you think people generally hide from God?

Can we ever really hide anything from God?

Perhaps we wish to portray a particular image so we hide one thing and embellish another. What kinds of things do people hide from each other?

Is concealing the whole truth the same as hiding?

Notes

Notes

How do some people use social media to conceal the truth, embellish, or portray an image?

Even "reality" television programs have portions scripted. What we're seeing may be fake. What reasons would we have for hiding the truth?

Is hiding parts of our lives bad? Why or why not?

Do you remember the story I shared in chapter thirteen? I disguised "hate" by simply renaming it "a strong dislike," and then proceeded to justify my emotions.

Yeah, I didn't convince God either. Rather, He convinced me of my sin. I sought forgiveness and became free.

Hiding has been occurring since the beginning of time. Read Genesis 3:1–10. What happened when Adam and Eve heard God coming?

What do you think could have been their motive to hide?

When and where are you most likely to hide something from God?

Jesus condemned a group who were hiding the truth from people Turn to Matthew 23. Jesus was talking to the crowds and the disciples about the scribes and Pharisees.

The scribes' and Pharisees' roles/jobs are described this way:

Scribes: Lawyers and teachers of the law. They weren't a religious sect, but a class of professional scholars. Their expertise in explaining the law and applying it to everyday circumstances allowed them to hand down legal decisions.

Pharisee: These were members of a Jewish religious sect, the most prominent group among the religious leaders. They emphasized the importance of keeping God's rules.[43]

The gospels frequently list the two together. The Pharisees advised the people, and the scribes interpreted the text or situation.

Read Matthew 23:5 and fill in the missing words. Referring to the religious officials, Jesus said, *All their works (deeds) they do* _____.

In fact, in this chapter we learn that Jesus used strong language to describe these leaders. He said, *"Woe to you."* Woe means "God's judgment, grief, and denunciation."[44]

How many times did Jesus say *woe*? _____

The scribes and Pharisees appeared to be godly. But Jesus knew their true motives and thoughts. Circle how Jesus portrayed the scribes and Pharisees:

You study very hard.	You are hypocrites.
You look good from man's perspective.	You have wrong motives.
You do works to be seen by man.	You have a special place.

Jesus chastised the scribes and Pharisees and rebuked them for their sinful behavior. Onlookers were deceived. But God wasn't.

Notes

Match the religious leaders' sins to the references in Matthew 23. (Two have the same verse.)

vv. 1–3	v. 4	vv. 5–7
vv. 13–14	v. 15	vv. 16–22
vv. 23–24	vv. 25–28	vv. 29–34

_____ You tell them what to do but you don't do it.

_____ You inflict heavy burdens on the people with so many rules, but you refuse to help them.

_____ You strap leather boxes of Scripture to your arms and forehead to show off to others and appear righteous.

_____ You attend the feasts, but in your selfishness, you insist on the best seat.

_____ You exempt yourself from God's law.

_____ You "saved" a person but with a false salvation so that the person lived far worse than before.

_____ You looked for ways to break oaths.

_____ You are obsessed with petty rules but neglect what is really important: mercy, justice, and faith.

_____ You cleanse the outside to look good, but your "inside" is filthy.

_____ You murdered the prophets and felt yourselves worthy to sit in Moses' seat.

Turn to Luke 20:45–47. Jesus was talking to His disciples. What did Jesus warn them about?

What did Jesus say about their "long prayers?"

Read Romans 2:21–23 and summarize those verses.

Now read James 1:22. How does this verse compare to Romans 2:21–23?

How are we sometimes like the Pharisees?

Read 1 Samuel 16:7 and fill in the blank: *The Lord said to Samuel, "Do not consider his appearance or his height, for I have rejected him. The Lord does not look at the things people look at. People look at the _____ _____, but the Lord looks at th _____."*

How can a person's good works actually be sin?

Can you recall a time you inadvertently tried to hide something from God? Do you think that maybe you didn't see the situation as God saw it? How so?

We can fool people, but being honest with God is all that matters. He's the One that counts. Is God urging you to admit something to Him? Talk to God about these things. Ask Him to open your eyes so you can see what He wants you to see (Psalm 119:18).

In 1 Chronicles 28:9, King David gave his son life-changing advice. He said, *"My son Solomon, know the God of your father, and serve Him with a loyal heart and with a willing mind; for the Lord searches all hearts and understands all the intent of the thoughts."*

Notes

Notes

Based on what you just read, what was David's advice?

Hiding trading cards may not seem so wrong. But if we make the analogy to our spiritual lives, attempting to hide sin is wrong. Will could fool his mother. But we can't fool God.

The good news is that God will reveal any sin we've got tucked away and forgive us when we ask. We won't have to look downcast as Will did. We'll empty our pockets and look up to God who made the light to shine in our hearts (2 Corinthians 4:6).

What Meant the Most to You from Today's Study?

Application

- Listen to "Out of Hiding, Father's Song" by Steffany Gretzinger and Amanda Cook. https://www.youtube.com/watch?v=XFkDqQtfs0w
- Listen to "Here's my Heart, Lord" by Lauren Daigle. https://www.youtube.com/watch?v=WTDoDA-1lsE

Light from the Scriptures

O Lord, You have searched me and known me. You know when I sit down and when I rise up; you understand my thought from afar. You scrutinize my path and my lying down, and are intimately acquainted with all my ways. Even before there is a word on my tongue, Behold, O Lord, You know it all. You have enclosed me behind and before, and laid Your hand upon me. For You formed my inward parts; You wove me in my mother's womb. I will give thanks to You, for I am fearfully and wonderfully made;

Wonderful are Your works, and my soul knows it very well.

My frame was not hidden from You, when I was made in secret, and skillfully wrought in the depths of the earth; eyes have seen my unformed substance; And in Your book were all written the days that were ordained for me, when as yet there was not one of them.

Psalm 139:1–5, 13–16

Notes

※
The good news is that God will reveal any sin we've got tucked away and forgive us when we ask. We won't have to look downcast. We'll empty our pockets and look up to God who made the light to shine in our hearts.
※

~ 17 ~
The Effect Our Words Have

Focus: We shine when our words are used to bring healing and life.

Words which do not give the light of Christ increase the darkness.

~ Mother Teresa

> ANNE SULLIVAN IS BEST KNOWN FOR TEACHING HELEN KELLER how to communicate by using sign language and reading Braille. At only twenty years of age, she began working with Keller. In a matter of months, she taught Keller nearly 600 words and how to read Braille.
>
> Despite Anne's own limited sight, she remained Keller's teacher, and the two shared their story of triumph on the Vaudeville theater circuit.
>
> Sullivan died in 1936 at her home. At her funeral, which took place at the Washington Cathedral in Washington, DC, Bishop James E. Freeman said, "Among the great teachers of all time she occupies a commanding and conspicuous place . . . the touch of her hand did more than illuminate the pathway of a clouded mind; it literally emancipated a soul."[45]

Anne Sullivan's hands . . . *her words* . . . made a life shine.

We all know the power words carry. Maybe you've heard the adage "sticks and stones may break my bones, but words can never hurt me." Originated in 1892, it was meant to help those being bullied by insults. A better adage might be what a shy first-grade girl told her teacher. She had made up her own ending: Sticks and stones may break your bones but words can break your heart."[46] In an age of bullying, we recognize the harmful effects that words can have.

Despite their effects, hurtful words occur in nearly every social setting. They may be used intentionally or they can creep into the conversation in a subtle way. Our churches are not excluded.

During prayer time, we share details that shouldn't be shared, and we discuss them with people who, unbeknownst to us, listen with the intention of obtaining information.

It's likely we've watched children suffer through the pain of hurtful criticism and verbal insults. Perhaps we've personally experienced the heartache of insensitive, careless words. And maybe we regret that we've participated in gossip and criticism too.

When we shine the light on our inconsiderate words, we discover this truth: Words can ignite a fire that leaves lifetime scars.

Throughout this study, you'll read many references to both the danger and benefit of our words. Why do you think God gives so much guidance, instruction, and warning on this topic?

Read Proverbs 12:18. To what are hurtful words compared?

Ouch. Words — spoken, typed, or texted — can hurt deeply or bring emotional death. When have you been at the receiving end of verbal daggers? How did it make you feel?

Contrast hurtful words with a time when someone said something uplifting and kind. What was said and how did it make you feel? What, if anything, did it motivate you to do?

We have two choices. We can use our tongue as a weapon to bring destruction. Or by speaking words of life, we can choose to use our tongue as a weapon to strike down Satan's attempt to destroy a person's self-worth and purpose.

Notes

Read James 3:2–8. James, who most scholars believe is the half-brother to Jesus, essentially says that if a person says she's a Christian, then she needs to act like one. In James 3:5, he points specifically to one area. What did he single out?

James then compared the power of the tongue to two other powerful inanimate objects. Read James 2:3. What do people who work with horses put in a horse's mouth?

What is the purpose?

The other object is revealed in James 2:4. What guides a ship?

A bit and rudder are small tools, yet they possess great power and are capable of determining direction.

How are a bit and rudder like our tongue?

Raging fires are kindled from a single spark. Their flames have led to loss of homes, land, and lives. In a similar manner, a spark of the tongue can kill a relationship, ruin a reputation, and destroy a Christian's witness. In fact, Proverbs 16:27 tells us *a worthless man digs up evil, while his words are like scorching fire.* The tongue controls the direction our life takes and is capable of triggering emotional death.

Read again James 3:6 and fill in the missing words.

The tongue is a fire, the very world of iniquity; the _____ is set among our members as that which _____ _____, and sets on fire the course of our life, and is set on fire by hell.

Various translations say the tongue *stains, defiles,* or *corrupts.*

Ouch again.

Flip back to James 1:26–27. Fill in the missing words. *If anyone among you thinks he is _____, and does not bridle his tongue, but deceives his own heart, this one's _____ is useless.*

What do you think James meant when he wrote "this person is deceived"?

Yikes . . . an unbridled tongue makes our religion useless. What do you think that means?

In Luke 6:45 we read this: *His mouth speaks from that which fills his heart.* Our problem, therefore, isn't with our mouth; the problem lies with the condition of our heart and our relationship with Jesus.

Continue reading in James 3:8. What did James say our tongue is "full of"?

Most translations use "deadly poison." Psalm 140:3 describes another entity who has deadly poison. What reptile is used in this illustration?

Notes

Notes

A wicked person who uses harmful words is likened to the serpent. They both spew deadly poison.

Which of the following has the potential to poison another? Circle all that apply.

    Lying   Gossip   Exaggeration   Slander   Helpful criticism

Deadly poison kills the physical body; harmful words kill the soul.

Let's go a step further. Ephesians 4:29 tells us: *Do not let any unwholesome talk come out of your mouths, but only what is helpful for building others up according to their needs, that it may benefit those who listen* (NIV).

The word translated as unwholesome in this verse literally means "rotten." The ESV uses the word corrupt, and the RSV uses evil. The NLT presents the verse like this: *Don't use foul or abusive language. Let everything you say be good and helpful, so that your words will be an encouragement to those who hear them.*

Circle the words "foul" and "abusive." Today, abusive language is also considered a form of emotional abuse. Think about their definitions.

Abusive: Using harsh, insulting language; emotional cruelty.

Foul: Offensive, obscene, abusive, detestable, vulgar or insulting language.[47]

For some people, using foul or abusive language is a habit. Maybe they grew up with this type of language in the home or live in a culture where this kind of language is socially acceptable. Do you struggle in these areas? Why or why not?

How can a foul mouth detract from a Christian's witness?

Do you think gossip qualifies as a form of abuse? Why or why not?

Notes

Skip ahead to James 4:11. In your opinion, is speaking evil on the same level as or worse than a gossiper or someone who is slanderous or a backstabber?

Match each of the following references to its best summary.

   __ Proverbs 10:19   A. Talking a lot generates a greater chance to sin.
   __ Proverbs 11:13   B. A gossip reveals secrets.
   __ Proverbs 20:19   C. Gossipers are busybodies.
   __ Timothy 5:13   D. Avoid people who gossip/talk too much.

Talking too much can lead to sin. But how, do you think, can a person "participate" in gossip without saying a word?

Let's continue with another thought — one that should be put to death. Read Colossians 3:8–9.

Slanderers comes from the Greek word *diaboloi*, which means, "accusers, defamers, those who maliciously attack another's good name, humiliate or malign others. They speak falsehoods for the purpose of damaging others."[48]

Conviction hurts, but if dealt with, also brings healing.

In what area(s) do you struggle the most?

   Gossip   Idle talk   Mean-spirited conversation

   Slander   Abusive speech

Notes

Let's wrap up the harsh reality of our words with Ephesians 4:31. This verse contains a list of worldly sins that stem from a hostile heart. What are these sins?

Depending on the translation you're using, you may have seen a variety of synonyms. The NIV substitutes the words *brawling* and *slander* for *evil speaking*. The NASB uses **clamor**. The NLT uses *harsh words* and calls all these words evil.

But here's hope. Used in the right way, our tongue can become a powerful tool to bring light to the darkness. Author and pastor Charles Spurgeon said, "If there were no gratified hearers of ill reports, there would be an end to the trade of spreading them." Sounds like a good place to start.

Psalm 39:1 is another great place to begin. What does King David write that he will strive to do?

When do you find it most difficult to muzzle your mouth or bridle your tongue?

What do you think would happen if the people with whom you work and socialize, prayed Psalm 39:1 before beginning the day?

In the movie *Bambi*, Thumper's mother reminds him, "If you can't say something nice, don't say anything at all." This Disney movie is worth watching for no other reason than to hear those words of wisdom.

The acronym T.H.I.N.K can be helpful too. Ask yourself if it is:

- T- True
- H- Helpful
- I- Inspiring
- N- Necessary
- K- Kind

Proverbs 15:1–4 tells us: *A gentle answer turns away wrath, but a harsh word stirs up anger. The tongue of the wise adorns knowledge, but the mouth of the fool gushes folly.* **The eyes of the Lord are everywhere, keeping watch on the wicked and the good.** *The soothing tongue is a tree of life, but a perverse tongue crushes the spirit* (NIV, emphasis added).

At first glance, Proverbs 15:3 (in bold) appears out of place. But it's a very fitting reminder that God hears the way we choose to speak. Two different ways of speaking are described; one is wicked, the other is good.

Compare these two by listing the words used in Proverbs 15:1–4 in the appropriate columns.

Wicked	Good
_____	_____
_____	_____
_____	_____
_____	_____
_____	_____
_____	_____
_____	_____

Read Ephesians 4:29. List the kinds of words we need to speak.

Notes

Notes

Think back on a time you made a big bowl of popcorn and salted it. Why did you add salt? What did the salt do to the popcorn?

Read Colossians 4:6. What does our speech need to be seasoned with?

As Christians, we have the opportunity to flavor another person's life. Match these references to the amazing Scriptures that show our great potential to bring healing and life:

__ Job 4:4	A. She opens her mouth in wisdom, and the teaching of kindness is on her tongue.
__ Proverbs 12:25	B. Anxiety in a man's heart weighs it down, but a good word makes it glad.
__ Proverbs 15:4	C. Pleasant words are as a honeycomb, sweet to the soul, and health to the bones.
__ Proverbs 15:23	D. Your words have helped the tottering to stand, and you have strengthened feeble knees.
__ Proverbs 16:24	E. A soothing tongue is a tree of life.
__ Proverbs 31:26	F. A man has joy in an apt answer, and how delightful is a timely word!
__ Colossians 4:6	G. Let your speech always be gracious, seasoned with salt, so that you may know how you ought to answer each person.

We're imperfect vessels who will make mistakes and sometimes fail to think before we speak. Thankfully, we can confess our mistakes to God and start over. We can ask God to help us bring health, healing, and life to others by using our words the way He would want.

Psalm 119:130 tells us *the unfolding of our words brings light to others*. Whose life can you light up today?

What Meant the Most to You from Today's Study?

Application

- Host a popcorn and movie night for the children in your life. Serve plain popcorn. Ask those eating to describe it (plain, bland, tasteless). Then sprinkle salt or powdered butter flavoring on the popcorn. Emphasize: Like salt that flavors popcorn, our words can flavor another person's life. Next, put on the Disney movie Bambi. Thumper learns an amazing lesson in this Disney classic.

- Write a message on a sticky note and leave it for your child, friend, roommate, or spouse to find. Suggestions are:

  - I believe in you!
  - You make me smile!
  - The world is better because you're in it!

- Listen to "Words" by Hawk Nelson. https://www.youtube.com/watch?v=anVweXDcxhA

Light from the Scriptures

The law of the Lord is perfect, restoring the soul; The testimony of the Lord is sure, making wise the simple. The precepts of the Lord are right, rejoicing the heart; the commandment of the Lord is pure, enlightening the eyes. The fear of the Lord is clean, enduring forever; The judgments of the Lord are true; they are righteous altogether. They are more desirable than gold, yes, than much fine gold; Sweeter also than honey and the drippings of the honeycomb. Moreover, by them Your servant is warned;

In keeping them there is great reward. Who can discern his errors? Acquit me of hidden faults. Also keep back Your servant from presumptuous sins; Let them not rule over me; Then I will be blameless, And I shall be acquitted of great transgression. Let the words of my mouth and the meditation of my heart be acceptable in Your sight, O Lord, my rock and my Redeemer.

Proverbs 19:7–14

> **Notes**
>
> When we shine the light on our inconsiderate words, we discover this truth: Words can ignite a fire that leaves lifetime scars.

❦ 18 ❦
Brilliant Wisdom

Focus: We shine when we have wisdom.

If you lack knowledge, go to school.
If you lack wisdom, get on your knees!
Knowledge is not wisdom.
Wisdom is the proper use of knowledge.

~ Vance Havner
Author and Preacher

I URGENTLY NEEDED TO MAKE A VITAL DECISION REGARDING my mom's health care and rehabilitation options. With only days until decision time, I was overwhelmed with the choices — and the fear of making the wrong decision. On a Sunday night, my heart boldly called out to God:

"I need wisdom to know what to do! I boldly come before the throne of grace asking for wisdom that You said You'd give. I'm going to pray intentionally and with purpose until You give me an answer. But more than that, You must also provide my mom with the same wisdom so we're in complete agreement. And we must have it now."

My prayer continued for two days. Then I visited my mom in the hospital. After praying together, Mom smiled and said, "Last night I had a dream. I was in a room with a large picture window. Fall flowers were growing in the garden, and I could see birds eating at the feeders. I commented to the nurse that my daughter would come decorate the sterile-looking room and make it more attractive."

My mom looked into my eyes and said that God was showing her where she needed to go. God gave both my mother and me the wisdom to make the right choice. We hugged and cried tears of joy. The wisdom God provided filled us with peace.

After this experience, I wondered why I hadn't prayed boldly for wisdom in other areas of my life.

In many cultures, the owl represents wisdom. Because of its nocturnal vigilance, there's a deeper meaning to the symbolism of the owl. According to one Christian tradition, "owls represent the wisdom of Christ, which appeared amid the darkness of the unconverted."[49]

Wisdom, though, is more than a tradition; wisdom drives us toward success. James 1:5 tells us God is willing to give generous amounts of wisdom. Maybe you rationalize that God gives more to some and less to others when He doles out wisdom. More to the preachers and missionaries, for example.

When have you asked for wisdom but felt like you received confusion?

Read James 1:5. Fill in the missing words.

_____ *lacks wisdom, let him ask of God, who gives to all generously and without reproach, and it will be given to him.*

Anyone.

Now let's look at the complete package. Read Proverbs 2:6. What three things does God give?

Being informed and knowledgeable isn't the same as having wisdom. Knowledge and wisdom are defined this way:

Knowledge is "information gained through experience, reasoning, or acquaintance."

Wisdom is "the ability to discern or judge what is true, right, or lasting."[50]

The Greek word translated as wisdom is *sophia*, meaning knowledge as well as profiting through our challenges.[51]

Notes

Author and Bible commentator Warren Wiersbe, helps put this in perspective: "Knowledge enables us to take things apart, but wisdom enables us to put things together and relate truth to daily life."[52] Charles Spurgeon said, "Wisdom is the right use of knowledge. To know is not to be wise. Many men [and women] know a great deal, and are all the greater fools for it. There is no fool so great a fool as a knowing fool. But to know how to use knowledge is to have wisdom."[53]

There's an axiom that the gray hair on older women is a symbol of wisdom. But just because a woman is older, doesn't make her wiser; age and spiritual maturity aren't synonymous. Spending time with God each day is how we become spiritually mature and wise. In this way, a younger Christian woman can be spiritually wiser than her unbelieving elder. Any woman who chooses to leave God out of her daily life remains unchanged by Him. Annual birthdays don't change us — a relationship with Jesus does.

If you're a young woman, can you identify an older lady whom you believe is spiritually stronger and from whose wisdom you could benefit?

If you're an older woman, is there a young woman whom you feel is spiritually your equal? If so, what do you think has made the difference in her life?

Solomon is known for being the most famous wise person in ancient Israel. First Kings 4:30 tells us *Solomon's wisdom surpassed the wisdom of all the sons of the east and all the wisdom of Egypt*. Solomon is also credited with authoring the book of Proverbs — short statements based on experience and gathered over time — but there are others who were wise contributors.

Solomon wrote 3,000 proverbs, 1005 songs, and spoke on a wide range of topics.[54] He received wisdom because He asked God for it.

Read his prayer recorded in 2 Chronicles 1:7–12:

That night God appeared to Solomon and said to him, "Ask for whatever you want me to give you." Solomon answered God, "You have shown great kindness to David my father and have made me king in his place. Now, Lord God, let your promise to my father David be confirmed, for you have made me king over a people who are as numerous as the dust of the earth. Give me wisdom and knowledge, that I may lead this people, for who is able to govern this great people of yours?" God said to Solomon, "Since this is your heart's desire and you have not asked for wealth, possessions or honor, nor for the death of your enemies, and since you have not asked for a long life but for wisdom and knowledge to govern my people over whom I have made you king, therefore wisdom and knowledge will be given you. And I will also give you wealth, possessions and honor, such as no king who was before you ever had and none after you will have."

Solomon pinpoints the beginning of wisdom. Read Proverbs 9:10.

The _____ of the Lord is the beginning of wisdom and the _____ of the Holy One is understanding.

What do you think it means to fear the Lord?

Reverence. Grasping God's holiness. Seeing God for who He is, not a coddling God who changes to meet our desires as often as the wind blows, which is the watered-down version of God we often see in our culture.

Solomon then discloses how to have a successful life. Some of the proverbs may have been written early in Solomon's reign. As all imperfect humans do, Solomon experienced sinful temptations, and he succumbed to them. His sin and disobedience were the gradual decay which caused the downfall of his kingdom and reign (1 Kings). Many of the proverbs, then, may have been written as he recalled his mistakes and warned others to go another way.

On the next page, match the proverb to its reference.

Notes

Notes

___ Proverbs 8:11   A. *There is a way which seems right to a man, but its end is the way of death.*

___ Proverbs 8:35   B. *Commit your works to the L*ORD *and your plans will be established.*

___ Proverbs 14:12   C. *The naive believes everything, but the sensible man considers his steps.*

___ Proverbs 14:15   D. *He who finds me [wisdom personified] finds life and obtains favor from the L*ORD.

___ Proverbs 16:3   E. *Wisdom is better than jewels; and all desirable things cannot compare with her.*

Because of sin, there will always be conflict while on this earth. Wisdom, however, is the spiritual light that guides our thought process and consequent actions in all areas, including these:

- Finding boundaries with adult children
- Balancing activities
- Seeking medical treatment
- Sharing the gospel
- Maintaining productivity
- Cultivating and dissolving relationships
- Fulfilling your purpose
- Caring for an elderly parent
- Handling conflict
- Giving or seeking forgiveness
- Pursuing marital advice
- Striving towards financial freedom
- Investigating career options

In what area of your life do you need wisdom?

Ecclesiastes 8:1 tells us *a person's wisdom brightens their face and changes its hard appearance* (NIV). Maybe we all could use a makeover.

A right relationship with God is the beginning of wisdom. However, God's Word tells us that two things prohibit this connection.

First, read 1 Samuel 12:23. To not pray is _____.

Second, recall Psalm 66:18. God will not hear if I have _____.

Notes

Repenting of sin and communicating with God through prayer enables us to have a relationship with Him and be led by Him.

Why do you think confessing sin to God is difficult? Circle all that apply to you:

- I'm unsure of sin
- I'm embarrassed
- I'd have to stop and I don't want to
- I feel shame
- I'm comfortable in my sin
- Other_____

A friend of mine was in desperate times. I recommended she take her burdens to God and get help. In all transparency she replied, "I won't. I'm not that woman! I have ignored God and done things on my own for so long. I refuse to be a hypocrite and run to God only when I need help."

I listened as she ranted a bit longer. When she stopped I said, "Amen. That whole conversation was heard by God, and you can make it your prayer of confession — for being independent and self-reliant."

She did. She started fresh. With God leading, her life began to change.

Seek God. Don't run away in shame or guilt. Sprint as fast as you can into the arms of God in repentance. He is quick to forgive and longs to bring restoration.

Maybe right now you feel overwhelmed with the burdens of past guilt. Psalm 51 is an excellent chapter to read in its entirety, but verse ten gets straight to the point: *Create in me a clean heart, O God, and renew a steadfast spirit within me.*

If you're unsure of what could be prohibiting a relationship with God, recall Psalm 119:18 as a prayer: *Open my eyes, that I may behold wonderful things from Your law.* He will uncover what's hidden, permitting you to see.

Notes

God desires to provide us with the wisdom we need to illuminate our darkness. Then we'll radiate as described in Daniel 12:3: *Those who have insight will shine brightly like the brightness of the expanse of heaven, and those who lead the many to righteousness, like the stars forever and ever.*

Shine on . . . you're a star!

What Meant the Most to You from Today's Study?

Seek God. Don't run away in shame and guilt. Sprint as fast as you can into the arms of God in repentance. He is quick to forgive and longs to bring restoration.

Application

➢ My young granddaughter keeps a white owl on the bed in her room at my house. Each day I see it, I'm reminded to ask God for wisdom in handling the day's affairs. Owl stickers, an owl coffee mug, or an owl magnet can also be a reminder to ask God for wisdom.

➢ Listen to "The Perfect Wisdom of Our God" by Keith and Kristyn Getty.
https://www.youtube.com/watch?v=hSnzYnOe6kI

Light from the Scriptures

Acquire wisdom! Acquire understanding! Do not forget nor turn away from the words of my mouth. Do not forsake her, and she will guard you; Love her, and she will watch over you. The beginning of wisdom is: acquire wisdom; and with all your acquiring, get understanding. Prize her, and she will exalt you; she will honor you if you embrace her. She will place on your head a garland of grace; she will present you with a crown of beauty. Hear, my son, and accept my sayings and the years of your life will be many. I have directed you in the way of wisdom; I have led you in upright paths. When you walk, your steps will not be impeded; and if you run, you will not stumble. Take hold of instruction; do not let go. Guard her, for she is your life.

Proverbs 4:5–13

~ 19 ~
Becoming Polished

*The fact that I am a woman does not make me
a different kind of Christian,
but the fact that I am a Christian
makes me a different kind of woman.*

~ Elisabeth Elliot

Focus:
*We shine
when we embrace
our identity and
worth
as a woman
of God.*

> IN APRIL 2015 A POPULAR SKINCARE AND BEAUTY LINE shared this research:
>
> Dove asked women worldwide to walk through one of two doorways. One door was labeled "Beautiful" and the other door was "Average." A shocking 96 percent of the women walked through the Average door; just 4 percent considered themselves beautiful.
>
> One participant said, "Beautiful, to me, is too far out of reach." Another woman confessed, "It was comforting to see these signs, and to have to choose, and be self-conscious of how you perceive yourself and if it lines up with how the rest of the world perceives you."
>
> An American participant added, "Am I choosing because of what is constantly bombarded at me and what I'm being told that I should accept? Or am I choosing because that's what I really believe?"[55]

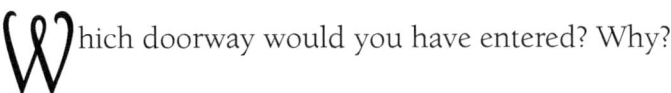hich doorway would you have entered? Why?

At one time or another, most of us have wrestled with what it means to be a beautiful woman. We wonder if we're beautiful . . . enough. One participant in the survey said, "Knowing that it's your decision to feel beautiful is powerful. Once you realize that, no one can make you feel otherwise."

Notes

Do you agree that owning your beauty is powerful? Why or why not?

Many books and poems have been written expressing diverse ideas — many contradictory — about the role of women and their beauty. We'll look at only one book — God's Holy Word — and scrutinize one verse. God, who created women, can best define a woman's attributes, her role, and her overarching purpose as a female.

Our key verse is Psalm 144:12 from the KJV. Read it written here:

Our daughters may be as corner stones, polished after the similitude of a palace.

There's a lot packed into this short verse. God's verbiage is always perfect — deliberate and profound. Circle the words polished and corner stones.

We'll examine these words further, with the assistance of *The Treasury of David Commentary*. But first let's look at their definitions:

Polished   "shiny, as a result of being rubbed; accomplished, skillful, and refined"

Cornerstone   "something of basic importance; a basic element—the foundation"[56]

In Hebrew, *polish* means to make smooth; to cut with a chisel. There's a powerful connection between polished and cornerstone. In the context of our verse, a polished woman is likened or compared to the ornamental columns of a palace. A sculptor uses a chisel to sculpt the decorative features.

As we continue to study polished in the context of Psalm 144:12, we discover that godly women are:

Strong	Beautiful	Wise
Refined	Cornerstones[57]	

Bible commentator Matthew Henry put it like this:

> When women are adorned with the graces of God's Spirit, which are the polishing of that which is naturally rough, and "become women professing godliness" and purified and consecrated to God as living temples, they are polished after the similitude of the palace.[58]

Let's consider the characteristics of a godly woman more closely.

Polished Women Are Strong

How would you describe a palace column? Circle all that apply.

Weight-bearing	Supportive	Pristine
Unshakable	Dependable	Strong
Powerful	Other_____	

Columns hold structures up or serve as the foundation on which something else is held. A woman is likened to the column because of the emotional, mental, and spiritual strength that is essential to undergird others. Her spiritual strength also enables her to resist the temptation to believe she is anything less than worthy.

Satan uses social media, television, radio, magazines, and bad relationships to lie to us about our worth. Each of these can be a vehicle to directly or indirectly tell us we're:

too young	too old	not good enough
not smart enough	not pretty enough	not worthy of respect
boring	untalented	unfit

Satan's objective is to destroy a woman's self-worth, purpose, and identity. These lies are easy to believe. Only a strong, courageous woman can disregard the lies of the Enemy and choose to believe what God says about her. The more time we spend with God in Bible reading and prayer, absorbing the truth, the stronger we become.

To which lie do you succumb?

Polished Women Are Beautiful

A plain, wooden column can do its intended job to support. But a sculptor chisels away the rough wood to create something beautiful. The column's beauty reflects the pride and skill of the column maker. In a similar manner, our beauty — both inner and outer — reflects the skill of our Creator.

Recall Zechariah 2:8 that we read in chapter one. Those who belong to Christ are the apple of God's eye. The apple is the pupil of the eye. When we look into another person's eye, we see our reflection. Similarly, when God looks into our eyes, He sees His reflection — that of a Beautiful Creator.

What others see initially is outward beauty. What physical attributes do you consider to be your most beautiful?

Our physical appearance will change with age. But inner beauty is eternal.

Read Psalm 45:13. What does this verse say about a woman's inner beauty in addition to her external clothing?

Read 1 Peter 3:3–4. A beautiful woman is described as having a _____.

This woman exemplifies the fruit of the Spirit (described in chapter six) and shines with the love of God. Others are drawn toward her, and God is glorified.

Her mind is beautiful too. Bible commentator Arthur Jackson wrote that a woman's "inward virtues and endowments of her mind were her greatest ornament and glory."[59]

While we may not be skilled in everything, we're all accomplished and skillful at something.

In what way is your mind strong and knowledgeable? This isn't arrogance, so don't be embarrassed. Everything about you points back to the Creator.

Polished Women Are Wise

As discussed in chapter eighteen, the right use of knowledge makes a person wise.

Life is just tough sometimes. A wise woman knows her help comes from God, and in humility and dependence, she runs to Him to meet her every need. A lack of humility is a sin (Proverbs 8:13).

Pride creates the domino effect and leads to other sins: arrogance, self-sufficiency, self-reliance (Proverbs 16:18). God never intended for us to live separate from Him.

A wise woman believes that God does not tire from hearing from her. What are you dependent on God for today? What do you want to ask Him?

Polished Women Are Refined

Women go through the refining process the same way that gold or silver are refined.

After years of being squeezed under the heat and pressure of the earth, rock is broken and impurities, called dross, come to the surface. The refiner removes the dross, leaving behind gold and silver. The silversmith knows his work with the silver is completed when he can look into his work and see his reflection.

Women, too, are squeezed with the pressures of this life. The heat of adversities and pain bring dross to the surface, where God can scrape it off, removing the impurities.

Isaiah 48:10 tells us: *Behold, I have refined you, but not as silver; I have tested you in the furnace of affliction.*

What specific affliction is bringing you heat?

Notes

Can you identify dross that needs to come to your surface?

If yes, tell about it. If no, tell why you don't think so.

While we're being refined, God's truth can hurt. In Jeremiah 23:19 we read: *"Is not My word like fire?" declares the* LORD, *"and like a hammer which shatters a rock?"*

How is God's truth likened to a hammer?

But the process is worth it. Read Job 23:10. After the refining process is complete, we'll come forth as _____ _____.

God, the original goldsmith, allows heat and pressure to bring impurities to the surface. And like a refiner does with the dross, God scraps it off.

Diamonds, another precious metal, have a clarity characteristic, called inclusions. These don't go away. They make each diamond unique. We, too, will emerge as sparkling diamonds, gold, and silver — precious and beautifully unique. And just like the silversmith, God will see His reflection in us.

Polished Women Are Like Cornerstones

Scripture tells us Jesus is the Chief Cornerstone (Ephesians 2:20). Are you surprised that women are likened to a cornerstone? Why or why not?

The cornerstone is the foundation on which something else is constructed; it is both essential and valuable because it determines the position of the entire structure. What an honor to have this important position in the eyes of God. Women were designed by God to be the moral glue that bonds families, communities, and nations. God uses all women — single, married, widowed, or divorced — to make a difference in our culture.

With such importance placed on cornerstones, we can conclude that as godly women likened to a cornerstone, we are:

Influential	Worthy/Valuable
Respectable	Strong
Capable	Accomplished
Skilled	Competent
Qualified	Dignified

First Peter 2:9 tells us that we're God's special possession. Look in the Bible for women God used to change history: Jochabed, Rahab, Esther, Ruth, and many more. Choose to believe what God says about you and own the beauty that comes with this position.

Today, walk through the "beautiful" doorway. Others will see the Sculptor in you.

What Meant the Most to You from Today's Study?

Notes

Women, too, are squeezed with the pressures of this life. The heat of adversities and pain bring dross to the surface, where God can scrape it off, removing the impurities.

Application

- To help you remember the polished woman you are, use a small square box to represent a cornerstone. In it you might store a jewel or diamond. Wrap the box like a package and put a bow on it. Print "Polished Cornerstone" on top. Print one of the following adjectives on each of the four sides: Strong, Beautiful, Wise, and Refined. Look at the box as often as needed to remind you of the polished woman God says you are. (Credit: Yvonne Lehman)

- Create a Polished Woman alphabet. Write out each letter of the alphabet, and beside each letter write an adjective that describes you. For example, Active, Beautiful, Commendable, Delightful, Excellent, etc.

- Listen to "Diamonds" by Hawk Nelson. https://www.youtube.com/watch?v=Yf1ARbpB0gA

Light from the Scriptures

For this reason, since the day we heard about you, we have not stopped praying for you. We continually ask God to fill you with the knowledge of his will through all the wisdom and understanding that the Spirit gives, so that you may live a life worthy of the Lord and please him in every way: bearing fruit in every good work, growing in the knowledge of God, being strengthened with all power according to his glorious might so that you may have great endurance and patience, and giving joyful thanks to the Father, who has qualified you to share in the inheritance of his holy people in the kingdom of light.

Colossians 1:9–12 NIV

❦ 20 ❦
Transforming Our Thoughts

Watch your thoughts for they become words. Watch your words for they become actions. Watch your actions for they become habits. Watch your habits, for they become your character. And watch your character, for it becomes your destiny.

~ Laozi

Focus: We shine when we think on what's right and holy.

> MY THOUGHTS ENSNARED ME AND ROBBED ME OF SLEEP. I WAS consumed with fear of raising teens in a culture becoming more violent and social-media driven.
>
> I turned on the television hoping to become distracted. But the late-night news programs reporting crime only made me more panicked. Within minutes, a feeling of hopelessness and fear came over me. I shuffled through my nightstand drawer looking for a book or Bible, but instead found a picture I had cut from a magazine and placed there months before.
>
> The picture was of a lovely vase of daisies with these words written beneath the vase:
>
> *"Why are you downcast? Put your hope in God."*
> Psalm 42:11
>
> While Satan bellowed that all is lost in this hopeless society, God whispered, "Put your hope in Me."
>
> God's truth transformed my hopeless thoughts into peaceful ones. I turned off the light and went to sleep.

Medical doctors and researchers have discovered we have more control over our physical health than previously thought.

According to Dr. Caroline Leaf, 2–25% of human mental and physical illnesses are a result of our genes and environment. How a person actually thinks changes the brain and body. When we react by thinking negatively and making negative choices, the quality

Notes

of thinking suffers, resulting in poorer health. Toxic thinking changes the wiring of our brain in a negative way and wears down the brain and the rest of the body.[60]

We may need for our thought process to be transformed.

Legend has it that Spanish explorer Juan Ponce de Leon discovered a spring that restored the appearance of those who bathed or drank from it to their youthful beauty. The spring, in St. Augustine, Florida, has been made into a scenic attraction referred to as the Fountain of Youth. Although throngs of people visit, it's never been reported that an actual physical transformation has taken place.[61]

God's Word, however, tells us how a life-changing, long-lasting transformation happens. Read Romans 12:2 and fill in the missing words.

Do not be conformed to this world, but be transformed by the _____.

Transformation begins with an internal makeover in which we allow God to put our mind, heart, and attitude in sync with His.

As previously read in the quote at the beginning of this chapter, our character is revealed based on the thoughts we have about ourselves and others, including God. Ephesians 4:23 tells us: *Be renewed in the Spirit of your mind.*

What does "renew" mean to you?

Renew is defined this way: "to make like new: restore to freshness, vigor, or perfection."[62] Synonyms include *regenerate, revive, rebuild, repeat, resume, replace,* and *replenish.*

The Hebrew word translated as renew is *chadash*, used here as a verb meaning to "repair."[63]

What negative thoughts currently consume you?

In what ways do you need your thoughts to be repaired?

Notes

Second Timothy 1:7 is a life changer. To begin, read this verse and fill in the missing words. *God doesn't give _____ _____. God gives power, love, and _____ _____.*

Both the KJV and the NKJV use the term *sound mind*. Other translations use *self-discipline* (NIV), *self-control* (ESV), *discipline* (NASB).

Barnes' Notes on the Bible provides practical insight on a sound mind.

> The Greek word denotes one of sober mind; a man of prudence and discretion. The condition of a well-balanced mind is under right influences, meaning it sees things in their just proportions and relations.[64]

A sound mind is one of right thinking — not confusion. This is what we pray for ourselves, our spouse, children, friends, family — that God give us right thinking, discretion, and a well-balanced attitude. Then . . . what a wonderful world this would be, right? Maybe we can't change the world, but we can do an inner beauty makeover on ourselves. We can replace (or repair) negative thoughts with positive ones — truthful ones.

For example, let's go back to the opening story in which technology and social media brought hopeless thoughts. Watching television could initiate negative thoughts:

1. You're watching television. The woman in an adulterous affair appears to be having fun, wrapped up in the romance of a new or mysterious love. As you watch you become envious, wishing. . . .

2. You're viewing a commercial, but you miss the intended advertisement because you are focused on the fine home filled with an array of new appliances and décor. You decide. . . .

3. You're watching a reality TV show, and the women are talking negatively about someone. You think . . .

Notes

In each of the examples on the previous page, what negative emotions or thoughts might creep in?

As thoughts like these invade our minds, destruction isn't far away. How can negative thoughts lead to a chain of bad events?

We must take action to keep these negative thoughts at bay.

First, 2 Corinthians 10:5 tells us, *[Take] every thought captive to the obedience of Christ.*

The writer, Paul, is talking to the Corinthians about their defeatist worldview. He admonishes them to start thinking right and obey the Lord.

How can we take our perspective, ideas, and thoughts captive?

Second, read Philippians 4:7. Fill in the missing word.

God's peace will _____ *our hearts.*

The KJV uses the word *keep*. But most other translations use *guard*. The Greek word for guard is the verb *phroureo*, a military term that refers to soldiers guarding a town.[65]

What does it mean to guard your heart?

We guard our heart by immediately taking captive any negative, wrong thoughts. We guard our heart by meditating on God's Word. Then we can pray His words back to Him. For example:

Use this as your reference	To pray this:
2 Timothy 1:7	God, give me right thinking.
1 Corinthians 14:33	I'm confused. You're not the author of confusion. Remove all confusion and replace it with peace.
Psalm 118:6	Lord, everyone is against me. You said you are on my side. Help me hold it together.
Philippians 1:6	God, You said You began a good work in me. You won't leave me hanging . . . You will be faithful to complete it.
Isaiah 55:8–9	Father, I know that my thoughts are different than Yours. Change my thoughts to reflect Your desires.
Proverbs 3:5–6	Jesus, I'm not depending on myself and what I see or think is best. I acknowledge Your way and ask that You lead me.
Psalm 39:7	God, You're all the hope I have.
Romans 12:12	Father, help me be joyful in hope, patient in affliction, and faithful in prayer.

Notes

We must constantly be filling our minds with God's truth. When the devil says it's hopeless, for example, we can quote scriptures that confirm we *are* hopeful. We must ask the Holy Spirit to protect our thinking against false theologians, prophecies, and doctrine.

The apostle Paul tells us what to think about. Read Philippians 4:8 and list characteristics here:

_____ _____ _____

_____ _____ _____

_____ _____ _____

_____

Is there an attitude on this list, or otherwise, that does not come naturally? If so, which one(s)?

Notes

Which areas of your mind need to be transformed? Are there unhealthy attitudes? Are there lies from the Enemy? Is the right attitude dormant and needs to be revived? Write a prayer. Ask God to help you with these thoughts or attitudes.

In Isaiah 26:3 we read this: *The steadfast of mind You will keep in perfect peace, because he trusts in You.*

Trust God to give you right thinking and peace.

Read Proverbs 4:23 again and fill in the missing words.

Watch over your heart with all diligence, for from it flow the _____ _____.

GUARDED HEART ➡ TRANSFORMATION ➡ ABUNDANT LIFE

For our transformation, we won't be dipping into the Fountain of Youth; we'll be drinking in the Living Word of God and drenching ourselves in His truth. As God shines the light on our thoughts, we'll arise and shine (Isaiah 60:1 NIV).

What Meant the Most to You from Today's Study?

Application

> ➤ Use the time that you apply creams and makeup to your face to think about an internal transformation. For example, when applying lipstick, ask God to help you use your words to encourage others. If you use a cream for crow's feet every night, pray about a specific concern that nags you, like the noise that crows make. When applying under eye dark circle cream/makeup, ask God to reveal if there is any sin that needs to be confessed. (Credit- Lori Marett)

- This may sound redundant, but it is so effective. Take each of the verses from the chart in this chapter and write them on individual sticky notes. Attach the notes to your mirrors, refrigerator, car dashboard, or any place you will see them often. Let them serve as reminders to replace your negative thoughts with positive, truthful ones.
- Read *Switch on Your Brain* by Caroline Leaf.
- Listen to "Change My Heart Oh God" by Maranatha Music. https://www.youtube.com/watch?v=IlSmG-_eJTU

Light from the Scriptures

*I love the Lord, for he heard my voice; he heard my cry for mercy. Because he turned his ear to me, I will call on him as long as I live. The cords of death entangled me, the anguish of the grave came over me; I was overcome by distress and sorrow. Then I called on the name of the Lord: "Lord, save me!" The Lord is gracious and righteous; our God is full of compassion. The Lord protects the unwary; when I was brought low, he saved me. Return to your rest, my soul, for the Lord has been good to you. For you, Lord, have delivered me from death, my eyes from tears, my feet from stumbling, that I may walk before the Lord in the land of the living. I trusted in the Lord when I said, "I am greatly afflicted"; in my alarm I said, "Everyone is a liar." What shall I return to the Lord for all his goodness to me? I will lift up the cup of salvation and call on the name of the Lord. I will fulfill my vows to the Lord in the presence of all his people. Precious in the sight of the Lord is the death of his faithful servants. Truly I am your servant, Lord; I serve you just as my mother did; you have freed me from my chains. I will sacrifice a thank offering to you and call on the name of the Lord. I will fulfill my vows to the Lord in the presence of all his people, in the courts of the house of the Lord–in your midst, Jerusalem. Praise the L*ORD.

Psalm 116 NIV

Notes

For our transformation, we won't be dipping into the Fountain of Youth, but we'll be drinking in the Living Word of God and drenching ourselves in His truth. As God shines the light on our thoughts, we'll arise and shine.

Notes

*Focus:
We shine
when we run
with the goal
in mind.*

᎓ 21 ᎒

The Spiritual Race

*I press on toward the goal for the prize
of the upward call of God in Christ Jesus.*

Philippians 3:14 ESV

> WHEN MY YOUNGEST DAUGHTER WAS IN HIGH SCHOOL, SHE ran cross-country and track. She trained so that she could endure each race. I was her cheerleader, on the sidelines clapping and cheering. However, I joined her for her evening training runs around the neighborhood. I enjoyed the workout and bonding time with her.
>
> When her senior year arrived, we had trained for a half marathon and ran the race together. The following year, we ran another one. The third year, however, my daughter was away at college, so I ran without her.
>
> During that early, foggy morning, I had at least two hours to think while I trotted along. It was during this time that God began showing me mental pictures of what is required to victoriously cross the finish line in our spiritual race.

Maybe you've enjoyed a foot race or two. Perhaps you know all about walking the neighborhood path. Or maybe you've never run, jogged or walked at all . . . let alone paid money to enter a race that makes you sweat and ache all over.

Regardless, you and I are in a race — all Christ-followers are participants. We're in the most important race of all — the spiritual one. Our goal is to be a victorious finisher.

Hebrews 12:1 says: *Since we have so great a cloud of witnesses surrounding us, let us also lay aside every encumbrance and the sin which so easily entangles us, and let us run with endurance the race that is set before us.*

I drew six conclusions on race day when God gave me images of what it takes to be victorious. What's required for a foot race parallels what's needed for our spiritual race:

- Train regularly
- Throw off weight
- Identify the real enemy
- Live in community
- Persevere to the end
- Focus on the prize

Train Regularly

What is regular? Regular means "constituted, conducted, scheduled, or done in conformity with established or prescribed usages, rules, or discipline; orderly, methodical, regular habits."[66]

Becoming successful requires discipline and often requires regular training. A teen could be trained before she begins babysitting on her own. We become trained in higher education before beginning a profession. Training for a race involves months of daily commitment to exercise and strengthen muscles.

Likewise, the spiritual race requires a similar commitment. Because this race lasts a lifetime, we need to set aside time each day to open God's Word for training, discipline, strength, and instruction.

Second Timothy 3:16–17 tells *us all Scripture is inspired by God and profitable for teaching, for reproof, for correction, for training in righteousness; so that the man of God may be adequate, equipped for every good work.*

We make time for what's important. When and where is the best time for you to spend time alone with God?

Without regular time with God we may miss important instruction or opportunities. In fact, without regular time in God's Word, we could slow down, miss the right road, or pass out from exhaustion.

Notes

Throw off Weight

One of my weekly training spots was a dirt track around the circumference of a small neighborhood lake. A couple of times around the lake was equal to a mile. Most times, though, my deep thoughts caused me to lose count of the number of laps I'd run.

Rocks fixed the problem. I stored small rocks in my pants or jacket pocket or held them in my fist. When I completed a lap, I threw a rock into the lake. When all the rocks were gone, I was finished. However, the rocks in my fist or pocket were weighty, bulky, and distracting. By getting rid of them, I did away with these problems.

Sinful habits, wrong attitudes, or anxiety are rocks in our spiritual pockets, weighing us down.

David wrote Psalm 32:3–4. What words are used to describe how he felt physically?

When have you felt the weight of burdens pressing into you?

What emotion, thought, or attitude is currently weighing you down?

In Psalm 32:4 we read: *Your hand was heavy upon me.* The NLT says *"the hand of discipline"* was on him, and it was heavy. The KJV says, *"Thy hand."*

God's conviction will also feel heavy . . . like a burden we want to get rid of. He wants us to purge our body of poisonous sin and be clean. Maybe your rock resembles fear or worry. Write a prayer to God. Tell Him what is weighing you down. Ask Him to help you get rid of this weight.

Revisit Hebrews 12:1 on the first page of this chapter. Circle "lay aside every encumbrance and the sin which so easily entangles us." We can't be successful if we run into this day, next week, or a new season with weights we insist on stuffing into our pockets. Toss them into the lake of God's love and mercy.

Identify the Real Enemy

In my race, there were pleasant distractions along the way: a lovely sunrise, chirping birds, a gentle breeze. But there was also a snake in the middle of my path — flat-out, car-squished, dried-up dead. Unable to hiss. Powerless to strike.

Unlike the powerless snake, our Enemy — the devil — is alive and continues to hiss and spew his venom. His to-do list is summed up in three words. Having already studied John 10:10 in this study, you're sure to get the clear picture. What three words tell what the devil has come to do?

_____   _____   _____

First introduced in the Garden of Eden, Satan cleverly slithers his way into minds, distorting God's truth, hissing lies and casting doubt. He watches and waits for the opportunity to:

- Steal your dreams, strength, peace, and joy
- Kill your hope and your faith
- Destroy your confidence in God
- Destroy your work, your family, and your relationships

He may use the people around you, your family, coworkers, or those on the opposite side of the political spectrum, but Satan is the real enemy. Put on the armor of God and with God-confident strength, fight against Satan's attacks. Hebrews 4:12 tells us *the word of God is living and active and sharper than any two-edged sword.*

According to this verse, what do we fight with?

Notes

Notes

And to be clear, God's Word is sharper than what?

Use God's Word to slice up Satan's lies and cut him to the core. (Refer to Chapter 10 on how to use God's Word to fight.) Satan will be unable to hiss. Powerless to strike. Unable to spread his venom.

Do this often.

Live in Community

A little more than an hour into my race, I found myself jogging beside another woman. I was thankful I wasn't alone. The two of us stayed side by side for a short time, but then she slowed and dropped back behind me. I turned around and motioned for her to come back up beside me. She sped up and joined me again. We finished the race together.

Life is tough. We wouldn't want to trudge through difficult valleys without someone to help pull us up, encourage us, and just be with us. Neither would we want to reside on the mountaintop alone without someone to celebrate with or share the joy.

What kind of friend do you need now?

Put a checkmark beside any of the following that apply. Someone with whom I can:

Laugh _____   Pray _____   Encourage _____   Cry _____

Discuss _____   Plan _____   Be accountable_____

Read the following Scriptures and determine what action there is for you.

They were continually devoting themselves to the apostles' teaching and to fellowship, to the breaking of bread and to prayer. Acts 2:42

I can apply this personally by:

Let us consider how to stimulate one another to love and good deeds, not forsaking our own assembling together, as is the habit of some, but encouraging one another; and all the more as you see the day drawing near. Hebrews 10:24–25

I can apply this personally by:

Bear one another's burdens, and thereby fulfill the law of Christ. Galatians 6:2

I can apply this personally by:

Confess your sins to one another, and pray for one another so that you may be healed. James 5:16

I can apply this personally by:

Persevere to the End

The hills were strenuous and I was weary. It would certainly make sense to quit. Tears blurred my vision. My mind said, "I can't go on." But my heart said, "Don't quit."

The hills of hardship: financial uncertainty, physical and emotional pain, decisions, disappointments, or loss of hope. What hill(s) are you climbing?

In Philippians 3:14 Paul tells us: *I press on toward the goal for the prize of the upward call of God in Christ Jesus.*

Notes

How do you describe the phrase "press on"?

What are some synonyms? Antonyms?

Keep the momentum. The hill will level. The difficult times will get better; the relationships will heal. And you will leave the marathon of heartache running better than before, with a sense of relief and renewal.

Psalm 121:1–3 the psalmist says, *I will lift up my eyes to the mountains; from where shall my help come? My help comes from the L*ORD*, who made heaven and earth. He will not allow your foot to slip; He who keeps you will not slumber.*

Focus on the Prize

I saw the finish line. A sudden burst of energy allowed for a sprint. My family's cheers —words of confidence and encouragement — brought me to the finish line. I ran under the banner, across the drawn line, beside the large clock, and into the arms of my family. Finished. A competitor who completed her race and won the prize.

We also have both a great cloud of witnesses surrounding us and a finish line for the race on earth. Do not be discouraged by previous defeats. The victorious runner keeps her gaze focused on the prize.

One day we'll run into the arms of Jesus. And our prize will be hearing the Lord say, *"Well done, good and faithful servant"* (Matthew 25:23).

What Meant the Most to You from Today's Study?

Notes

Application

➢ Go on a walk or run with rocks in your pocket. Give each rock the name of something that is hindering you from completing your personal race. Then, lighten your load by throwing away rocks along the way, enabling you to cross the finish line.

➢ Listen to "Press on for the Prize Worth Fighting For" by Jamie Kimmett. https://www.youtube.com/watch?v=zRIyET9ykvs

Light from the Scriptures

Two are better than one because they have a good return for their labor. For if either of them falls, the one will lift up his companion. But woe to the one who falls when there is not another to lift him up. Furthermore, if two lie down together they keep warm, but how can one be warm alone? And if one can overpower him who is alone, two can resist him. A cord of three strands is not quickly torn apart.

Ecclesiastes 4:9–12

> ✠
> *A sinful habit, wrong attitude, or anxiety in the heart can be rocks in our spiritual pockets, weighing us down.*
> ✠

Notes

*Focus:
We shine when we obey God because we love Him.*

❧ 22 ❧
Compelled to a Life of Obedience

God wants you to enjoy the freedom which He gives you in every area; but the only way to obtain that liberty is through obedience. Obedience always brings blessing.

~ Charles Stanley

> BETH* NEEDED TO END A BEHAVIOR. SHE SHARES HER STORY of obedience:
>
> I grew up in church and was saved at a young age. Despite knowing that living together was wrong, I made a poor decision and moved in with my boyfriend anyway. I tried to explain myself to God, as if He didn't know my heart. It didn't change the sin. I felt disconnected from God as soon as my sin pattern began. Where was my peace? I knew He still loved me, but why couldn't I hear Him anymore? I knew the answer. Sin stood between us. I was convicted on a daily basis. I knew I had to make things right.
>
> The day came when both my boyfriend and I decided to be obedient to God and trust Him with our living arrangement. We wanted to do what was right. After several weeks of seeking God, He provided the strength for us to do the right thing. First, we found separate housing, and then we got married. Immediately, peace flooded my body! I know we went about things backward, but I also know now we are "right" with God. That sin can't weigh me down anymore. We are now able to attend worship without the shame and guilt of disobedience. God's peace and presence was such a blessing. But then God blessed us even more. We have a little baby boy on the way.
> *name changed

Maybe you can't relate to Beth's story. Can you, however, recall a time when you needed to be obedient and give up a sinful practice? If so, how did you handle it and what was the result?

Obeying God is comfortable, even easy when we agree with His plans or when obedience satisfies our desires or suits our purpose. It's also effortless to avoid the things that don't appeal to us. But when God asks us to do something we really don't want to do, that becomes problematic — and often the precursor to a strenuous testing period.

> LILLY* SHARES HER STORY OF OBEDIENCE. SHE NEEDED TO BEGIN . . . with a new attitude:
>
> My husband's ex-wife, Janet*, was dramatic, vindictive, and a master manipulator. For years Janet caused me to have heart palpitations and stress. As a newlywed, I received a phone call from Janet telling me she wished my husband, Bill*, was dead so she could collect his social security. Janet later told our daughter that Bill hated her. To say I disliked Janet is slightly embarrassing, probably not strong enough, but entirely true.
>
> Then one day I was reading God's Word. I read where Jesus said I must pray for my enemies — and I knew He meant that included Janet. I had routinely prayed for my family, for our daughter, for God's will, but never did it occur to me that I should pray for Janet.
>
> I wanted to be obedient, so I prayed — halfheartedly at first. But over time, and with God's help, it became easier to pray more genuinely. Peace flooded me as my own fear, anger, and hard feelings turned to compassion. Obedience is still a difficult choice. But when I choose to obey God, I am always rewarded with peace.
> *names changed

Reflect. When has there been a time you needed to take action and do something you initially didn't want to do?

What emotion or attitude do you need to surrender?

Sometimes, we unintentionally disobey God. For example, when an inappropriate emotion is not dealt with or an unexpected situation pops up and we don't respond very well. Other times, we choose to disobey His commands. Often, we're put in a

Notes

position that wasn't of our choosing — like when a child disobeys. Regardless, we must respond.

Love compelled the women who shared the stories above to obey God. Their love for Him outweighed their own desires. With God's help, they both resisted their sinful nature of pride and selfishness and chose to follow God's way. God received the glory, and He showered blessings of peace on them — not to mention a new baby for Beth.

Read Genesis 50:20. How can God make your difficult situation good, as in Lilly's case, when she didn't choose it?

Known as "a man after God's own heart," David left a legacy of surrendering himself to God. Although not sinless, he confessed his sins and habitually sought God. Read the following Scriptures.

It came about afterwards that David inquired of the Lord, saying, "Shall I go up to one of the cities of Judah?" And the Lord said to him, "Go up." (2 Samuel 2:1)

David inquired of the Lord, saying, "Shall I go up against the Philistines? Will You give them into my hand?" And the Lord said to David, "Go up." (2 Samuel 5:19)

David inquired of the Lord, saying, "Shall I pursue this band? Shall I overtake them?" And He said to him, "Pursue, for you will surely overtake them, and you will surely rescue all." (1 Samuel 30:8)

David inquired of the Lord, saying, "Shall I go and attack these Philistines?" And the Lord said to David, "Go and attack the Philistines and deliver Keilah." (1 Samuel 23:2)

What is David's pattern of behavior?

From just a few examples (there are many more) of David's dialogue with God, we get a glimpse into why King David's reign was a success. How would you explain his success?

David *inquired* of the Lord. God answered. David *obeyed*. And his obedience brought victory every single time.

We benefit greatly when we obey God. God's magnificent promises are overflowing. Read Deuteronomy 30:9–20 in its entirety, then we'll break it down.

In Deuteronomy 30:9, Moses wrote about the benefits that would be given to the people. What benefits did he mention?

Some are specific cultural benefits and wouldn't apply to us. But what can you surmise about how God would bless in today's culture?

Deuteronomy 30:10 tells us that some of God's blessings are conditional. What are the conditions? (Hint: They begin with "if.")

God is loving and patient. He continuously extends mercy. Even while the Israelites disobeyed Him in the wilderness, God took care of them. But God is also holy and just and may withhold certain blessings that were meant for us.

Deuteronomy 30:10 instructs us to keep God's *commandments* and *statutes*. What is the difference between these two words?

Notes

Notes

Statute: a written law that is formally created by a government

Command: an important rule given by God that tells people how to behave[67]

David takes seriously the command to obey God, as evidenced in this prayer to God, for his son, Solomon:

"Give my son Solomon a loyal heart to keep Your commandments and Your testimonies and Your statutes, to do all these things, and to build the temple for which I have made provision."

God established laws because He knows that living within these boundaries will lead to a successful life. When we choose to ignore God's laws or commandments, God, like a loving parent, disciplines us. And when we choose to obey, He blesses us. But either way, He is manifesting His love.

As Christ-followers, we've all been recipients of God's blessings. We're blessed with salvation and with religious freedom. Choosing to obey God's commands and live within the parameters He sets for us brings additional blessings. Beth and Lilly's blessings were a direct result of their obedience to God.

Now focus on Deuteronomy 30:11. A variety of synonyms are used among the various translations but this is the gist of the verse: *What I am commanding of you today is not too difficult to understand — or too far off* (beyond your reach).

Obeying God may *feel* difficult. Write why you think God says obedience is within our reach.

We grit our teeth, plead, and defend our disobedience, or simply fuss and cry. Eventually, though, we surrender and ask God to help us obey. How do you think God reacts when we choose to leave our comfort zone and step out in faith to obey?

Read the powerful verse found in Joshua 1:8 and fill in the missing words.

This book of the law shall not depart from your mouth, but you shall meditate on it day and night, so that you may be careful to do according to all that is written in it; for then you will make your way prosperous, and then you will __ _____.

Philippians 4:13 provides us with hope and encouragement. What does this verse say we can do with God's strength? Circle the best answer.

  Some things Nothing One thing All things

This includes being obedient and doing whatever God wants us to do. Time spent with God is individual and personal. Reading the Bible, praying, listening for God's quiet voice, listening to praise music, reading a psalm, or singing a hymn are some of the ways we spend time with God.

See more of God's promises for yourself. Match the reference to the verse.

___ *Blessed are those who hearthe word of God and observe it.*   A. Jeremiah 7:23

___ *He who has My commandments and keeps them is the one who loves Me; and he who loves Me will be loved by My Father, and I will love him and will disclose Myself to him.*   B. Luke 11:28

___ *Obey My voice, and I will be your God, and you will be My people; and you will walk in all the way which I command you, that it may be well with you.*   C. John 14:21

Fifteenth-century philosopher and theologian Saint Augustine said, "Wicked men obey from fear; good men, from love."[68]

Deuteronomy 30:12–14 tells us God's Word is near. Barnes' commentary says, "Ignorance of the requirements of the law cannot be pleaded."[69]

Notes

Read Deuteronomy 30:15–18. Two hearts — kinds of people — are compared. What is the result?

The Action	*The Result*
The person who obediently walks with God	
The person whose heart turns away from God	

Conclude by reading Deuteronomy 30:19–20. Summarize this passage.

Jesus is our ultimate example. He obediently went to the cross and set the pattern for us to be obedient. Take it one step at a time. These steps are steppingstones to great blessings. Even when His commandments seem outdated, unrealistic, or unreasonable, follow God faithfully. John 8:12 promises: *He who follows Me will not walk in the darkness, but will have the Light of life.*

Leave the results to God, and live in light!

What Meant the Most to You from Today's Study?

Application

- Stones and altars were used in the Old Testament to mark events and remember God's faithfulness. Today, make your own altar of remembrance to remind you God is faithful to His promises to help you and then bless you, when you keep His commands.
- Read the Nancy Leigh Demoss book *Choosing Forgiveness*.
- Listen to "Trust and Obey" by Big Daddy Weave. https://www.youtube.com/watch?v=k-LdHCuo5-Y

Light from the Scriptures

I will bless the Lord at all times: His praise shall continually be in my mouth. My soul makes its boast in the Lord; let the humble hear and be glad. Oh, magnify the Lord with me, and let us exalt his name together! I sought the Lord, and He answered me and delivered me from all my fears. Those who look to Him are radiant, and their faces shall never be ashamed. This poor man cried, and the Lord heard him and saved him out of all his troubles. The angel of the Lord encamps around those who fear Him, and delivers them. Oh, taste and see that the Lord is good! Blessed is the man who takes refuge in him! Oh, fear the Lord, you His saints, for those who fear him have no lack! The young lions suffer want and hunger; but those who seek the Lord lack no good thing. Come, O children, listen to me; I will teach you the fear of the Lord. What man is there who desires life and loves many days, that he may see good? Keep your tongue from evil and your lips from speaking deceit. Turn away from evil and do good; seek peace and pursue it.

Psalm 34:1–14 ESV

Notes

God established laws because He knows that living within these boundaries will lead to a successful life. When we choose to ignore God's laws or commandments, God, like a loving parent, disciplines. And when we choose to obey, He blesses. But either way, He is manifesting His love.

❦ 23 ❦
Confrontation: If, When, How

Focus:
We shine
when
in the midst
of confrontation.

This is one of the marks of a truly safe person: they are confrontable.

~ Henry Cloud
Author

> I sealed the envelope, put my stamp on it, and placed the letter in the mail.
>
> I wish I'd known then what I know now. I would've grabbed my words right back out of that mailbox!
>
> I believed the confrontational letter was a plea to put an end to unchristian behavior. Never intending to be judgmental, I truly thought my words would be contemplated and accepted as truth. But the opposite happened.
>
> I should've done things differently. I failed on many levels in choosing how and when to confront.

Has something like that ever happened to you? My failed attempt was decades ago, and for a little while, I thought I would avoid confrontation forever — until I discovered what confrontation is and what it isn't.

Relationships of all kinds can lead to disagreements or differences of opinion. Conflict is a part of life. Maybe you've wondered:

- Should confrontation be avoided?
- Will it start a quarrel?
- How do I know if confrontation is too abrasive?
- Will confrontation damage the relationship?
- Does confronting someone make it appear I think I'm better?

Let's establish what confrontation means both from a secular perspective and a biblical one. One secular source defines it this way:

> Confrontation implies hostility, although like a fight, a confrontation can involve actual violence, or just a clash of words. It often refers to a military encounter involving opposing armies. This meaning became popular after the Cuban Missile Crisis in 1963. Before that, *confrontation* was used to mean "bringing two opposing parties face to face."[70]

Do you agree that confrontation is usually aggressive or hostile? Why or why not?

Does choosing to be gentle (as opposed to aggressive) mean a person is weak?

Confrontation, or the act of confronting, can be defined this way: "to face especially in challenge: oppose."[71]

Opposition and confrontation arise throughout God's Word. The word rebuke, for example, is used throughout the Gospels. Let's look at one verse in particular. Read 2 Timothy 4:2 in the different versions.

Preach the word; be ready in season and out of season . . .

   . . . reprove, rebuke, exhort, with great patience and instruction. (NASB) (KJV)

   . . . correct, rebuke and encourage-with great patience and careful instruction. (NIV)

   . . . reprove, rebuke, and exhort, with complete patience and teaching. (ESV)

   . . . convince, rebuke, exhort, with all longsuffering and teaching. (NKJV) (RSV)

   . . . correct, confront, and encourage with patience and instruction. (CEB)

Most versions use *rebuke*, but one uses the verb *confront*.

Notes

Notes

Barnes' *Notes on the Bible* clarifies rebuke:

> In the *New Testament* the word is used to express a judgment of what is wrong or contrary to one's will, and hence, to admonish or reprove. It implies our conviction that there is something evil, or some fault in him who is rebuked. The word in this verse rendered "reprove," does not imply this, but merely that one may be in error, and needs to have arguments presented to convince him of the truth. That word also implies no superior authority in him who does it. He presents "reasons, or argues" the case, for the purpose of convincing. The word here rendered rebuke, implies authority or superiority, and means merely that we may say that a thing is wrong, and administer a rebuke for it, as if there were no doubt that it was wrong.[72]

Similarly, the *Jamison Bible Commentary* defines reprove as [to] "convict, confute."[73]

Whether we use rebuke, confront, oppose, or reprove, 2 Timothy 4:2 tells us how to approach a person with encouragement, patience, instruction, or teaching.

Are you comfortable with confrontation, or do you choose to avoid it? Do you actively steer clear of people with whom you might be in disagreement? Why or why not?

What makes you more uncomfortable, confronting another or being confronted?

Although my motivation for sending my letter was pure, I made some mistakes. Since then, I'm learning:

- Accountability is based on a trusting relationship.
- More time in prayer may be necessary to avoid reacting too quickly.
- Words must be chosen carefully.
- Love must be the motivation.
- Confrontation may not be the right approach.
- God's timing is an important factor.

The Bible tells us how to confront, oppose, or rebuke another, because in many instances, confrontation is necessary.

Accountability

Accountability between two people is based on a trusting, secure relationship with each other. After my confrontation, the relationship ended. But in hindsight, I realize the relationship didn't end because of a letter I wrote. I know now that a caring relationship had never begun.

Read Matthew 14:13–21. This may be a familiar story but let it remind you about how Jesus *felt* toward the crowd. What did He provide them with?

It may not be possible to establish a relationship with someone we must correct or confront. But as a rule, it's more effective when the person knows we're coming from a place of concern and care.

Think back to a time you were in a confrontation. Was there a confirmed relationship? Explain the outcome.

Pray

Many times we pray about big, life-changing events, but, we sometimes respond impulsively when the need arises to correct a person. It's important that we step back, take a breath, and pray first.

Read Philippians 4:6. What can we pray about? Cross off the one that is wrong:

    Small Stuff   Big Stuff   No Stuff   All Stuff

Generally speaking, when are you reluctant to pray?

Notes

Talking with another person about a sensitive subject, especially one that may provoke a defensive reaction, requires urgent prayer, particularly if the subject is time sensitive. In prayer, ask God to:

- Prepare the heart of the person you'll be confronting
- Provide you with understanding
- Give you the right words
- Go before you to establish His will

Choose Words Carefully

Read 1 Timothy 4:13. Fill in the missing word. *Until I come, give attention to the public reading of Scripture, to _____ _____ and teaching.*

Most translations use the word *exhortation*. The Greek word translated as exhortation means to "come alongside and help."[74] It involves comforting someone with strength and encouragement. Correction conveys the same idea. We come alongside a person to give counsel and show how the Scriptures relate to the situation.

In this way, how are encouragement and confrontation related?

Read and summarize Galatians 6:1.

Read and summarize 2 Timothy 2:25.

There is a time to oppose or confront, but these verses tell us it should be done in a particular way — or with something. What is it?

Teachers think about the best way to help their students understand, and lawyers think about the best way to expose the truth. Likewise, we need to think carefully about the words we use so that understanding, reconciliation, and conviction takes place. Proverbs 12:18 tells us *there is one who speaks like the piercings of a sword, but the tongue of the wise promotes health.*

Our goal must be to promote spiritual health and reconciliation to God.

Love Must Be Our Motivation

Recall the story of the Samaritan woman, found in John 4:1–42, and in chapter four of this book. Jesus' journeys were strategic. In this case, He met a woman at a well. He spoke to her personally and gently convicted her of sin.

What was her reaction to His gentle rebuke?

During Jesus' ministry on earth, hearts were changed, and bodies were healed. The scribes and Pharisees observed Jesus' actions and tried to trap Him in a lie or sacrilegious behavior. Jesus was honest and direct when He confronted the Pharisees for being hypocritical and judgmental (Matthew 23).

However, He still loved them.

Nicodemus was one of these Pharisees, yet after the conflict with Jesus, he later believed that Jesus was the Messiah. (See John 19.)

Confrontation should flow out of humility and a genuine desire to help another person be restored. It should not be a means of retaliation or motivated by out an "I told you so" attitude.

Read 2 Timothy 2:23–24. What produces quarrels?

This is the question we must ask ourselves: Is confrontation foolish and a waste of time? When we confront someone in love with the intent of restoration, then confrontation is not foolish. Confronting a person for a sinful attitude or behavior may be necessary for restoration or for their spiritual growth. From this perspective, confrontation, done properly, shows love. Keep in mind, though, a person's response is between her and God.

Is Confrontation Always the Right Thing to Do?

We need to ask God if we should say anything at all. Not every person will respond or benefit from a confrontation, especially if there are other spiritual, emotional, or mental issues standing in the way or if the person doesn't understand what you're trying to convey.

Jesus didn't waste time addressing every wrong action or thought. When the soldiers came to arrest Him in the Garden of Gethsemane, He didn't correct them or defend Himself (Matthew 26).

Once I was with a group of women from various Christian denominations. One woman criticized my denomination. It was snarky and out of context, and I was surprised by her harshness.

I prayed the words of James 1:5 for several days, asking God for wisdom to know what to do. *Should I confront her about her hurtful words and watered-down theology?* Over the next few days, I felt God leading me to stay quiet. We don't have to argue every point, especially about personal preferences in worship or the nonessentials. The incident was never brought up again.

Spend some time in prayer asking God if confrontation is the wisest choice. He will lead you.

Timing Is Important

If God gives the green light and opens the door for correction to take place, He will show you when to go. Meeting with a person after an extra-long, stressful day at work may not be the best time. Proverbs 27:14 tells us this: *He who blesses his friend with a loud voice early in the morning, it will be reckoned a curse to him.*

What do you think this verse implies?

Recall a time someone confronted you. How did you feel? Was the issue resolved? Why or why not?

We can pray for God's stamp of approval on all our words — written, typed, or spoken in confrontation.

What Meant the Most to You from Today's Study?

> *Accountability between two people is based on a trusting, secure relationship with each other.*

Application

- Listen to "Open Our Eyes" by Maranatha Music.
  https://www.youtube.com/watch?v=oZsZkB-HcyE

Light from the Scriptures

You will light my lamp; the Lord my God will enlighten my darkness. For by You I can run against a troop, by my God I can leap over a wall. As for God, His way is perfect; the word of the Lord is proven; He is a shield to all who trust in Him. For who is God, except the Lord?

And who is a rock, except our God? It is God who arms me with strength, and makes my way perfect. He makes my feet like the feet of deer, and sets me on my high places. He teaches my hands to make war, so that my arms can bend a bow of bronze. You have also given me the shield of Your salvation; Your right hand has held me up, Your gentleness has made me great. You enlarged my path under me, so my feet did not slip.

Psalm 18:28–36 NKJV

Notes

~ 24 ~
Activity Versus Busyness

Focus: We shine when we're balancing activity with rest.

Rest time is not wasted time. It is economy to gather fresh strength . . . . It is wisdom to take occasional furlough. In the long run, we shall do more by sometimes doing less.

~ Charles Spurgeon

I WATCHED THEM SCRAMBLING IN THE WOODED PART OF MY yard. Dozens of squirrels all moving around like they couldn't make up their minds about what to do, how fast to move, or where to go. They dug busily in the ground, scurried up trees, and chased one other.

Except for one.

This squirrel sat motionless on a short limb — twelve inches or so — protruding from the side of a tall oak tree.

Poor thing.

Then again, maybe he wasn't a sad case at all. I wondered if he deliberately put himself there.

I watched a few seconds longer.

My life resembles this scene, some days.

To which of the squirrels above can you best relate this week — the ones scrambling about or the one being still?

Is there a difference between being busy and being active? How would you compare and contrast them?

The *English Oxford Living Dictionary* defines activity:

Activity: the condition in which things are happening and being done
Busy: having a great deal to do[75]

Synonyms for activity include:

pursuit	venture	action	occupation	undertaking
interest	enterprise	project	hobby	diversion
pastime	scheme	recreation	entertainment	deed

The word is derived from the Latin root word "act," meaning "do."

Compare the synonyms for busy:

overworked	occupied	hectic	crowded	hard-pressed
absorbed	engrossed	preoccupied		

Interestingly, the word *busy* is derived from an old English word meaning "careful or anxious." Over the centuries, the meaning expanded to include "anxiousness, being active in that which does not concern one (busybody), and prying."

Compare the synonyms of *busy* and *activity*. Which list leans towards being negative?

What's "busy" to one is simply "being active" to another. There are many stages in one's life; some of those stages require more activity than others.

An older woman shares this perspective:

> At this stage in my life, which is less required-responsibility toward others, I am blessed to be "active." I'm active because I require myself to stay busy. Even in my busiest time when raising children, taking care of husband and home, working, writing, running a conference, I was active in church, therefore communing with God. However, doing church work can be busyness too.

Busyness is associated with anxious behavior and being a busybody. First Thessalonians 4:11 tells us: *Make it your ambition to lead a quiet life and attend to your own business and work with your hands, just as we commanded you.*

The NLT words it this way: *Make it your goal to live a quiet life, minding your own business and working with your hands, just as we instructed you before.*

The implication is to do what's most important and avoid the distraction of being involved in everybody else's business. While a busybody is usually involved with other people, anxiousness is a state of mind and can happen while we're alone. Even when our bodies momentarily stop — like when we're stopped at a red light — our mind continues to move fast-forward, looking ahead to the next task.

Describe a time when your body was idle but your mind was busy.

Which best describes your current season of life?

- ❏ I am not too busy. I make time for rest and play. My work, home, and projects are well-managed. I feel happy.

- ❏ I often don't know if I'm coming or going. Sometimes I have difficulty sleeping because I think about the day's activities and what's coming the next day. I'm overwhelmed and just plain tired.

The research on busyness is massive. Depending on which report you read, you can find equal benefits to working more or less. The *Harvard Business Review* reported in the article "Busyness in America" that people who work all the time feel they are sought after, which enhances their perceived status and makes them feel important.[76]

How does being busy promote one's self-esteem?

How does a desire to improve our self-concept through busyness affect the following areas of life? (Begin on the next page.)

Career:

Notes

Work around the home:

Caring for children or others:

Being involved in church or community activities:

Sometimes we choose to be too busy, but at other times, although we reject the pressure to schedule too much, we're left with no choice. It's the hand we're dealt for a particular time and season.

An article written for *Focus on the Family* says our culture rewards us for being busy. For moms especially, there is an expectation they're supposed to be busy. When they adapt to this expectation, they are emotionally satisfied.

> Moms learn over time that when they are very busy, they don't have to question themselves at the end of the day about whether they got enough done. But if they have a lot of free time, they start to question whether they are being selfish or lazy and miss the sense of accomplishment from a couple days ago when they were overworked. Moms should be proud of all they accomplish during a busy, complicated day — but they should also be proud of getting some rest.[77]

There are other caregivers too. Adult children caring for aging parents are equally as busy. Grandparents actively involved in their grandchildren's lives discover they've become busy balancing activities and travel. Single adults can become busy with church and community events. One single woman reported

Notes

that often her friends call for support and help with babysitting, pet sitting, or housesitting, because they assume she has nothing to do. Finding it difficult to say no, she becomes overwhelmed with too much to do.

The reasons for busyness range from a temporary situation to a chosen habit. What's important, though, is that we get a sense of what busyness looks like, how it affects us and the people we love, and how we can best deal with it.

Read Luke 10:38–42.

I like Martha. A lot.

She was a friendly, service-driven, problem-solving gal. Her motivation for what she did flowed from a caring, compassionate heart and her gift of hospitality.

What was Martha doing in this passage?

How does your Bible version describe Martha's state of mind?

Where did Martha go wrong? Was it being the hostess? Was it about not "being still"? Was this more about her attitude toward Mary?

How did Jesus respond to Martha?

Picture the moment. When Jesus spoke her name twice, He was displaying intimacy and friendship. He used a gentle reproof and a special tenderness in the repetition of her name.[78]

If Jesus wasn't implying that hospitality and service weren't worthy and a good calling, what was He saying?

Jesus said Mary had chosen what was better. What was Mary doing? What was her attitude?

Write your name in the blank twice, just like Jesus used Martha's name twice.

_____, _____, *you are distracted and worried with many things.*

How did filling your name in the blank make you feel?

It's not wrong to be active and use our gifts. However, we need to balance our time with rest — resting the body and the soul.

People, families, and situations are unique. Whether you're married, single, raising children, or retired, there's the potential to be overly busy with a never-ending to-do-list. Busyness does more than make our bodies physically exhausted. Busyness affects us emotionally and can lead to:

- a feeling of being overwhelmed
- stress
- exhaustion
- sleep deprivation
- mental distraction
- burnout[79]

When, if ever, have you experienced one or more of these?

Notes

Notes

More than a decade ago, my oldest daughter taught me a valuable lesson:

> Her contrary, argumentative attitude prompted me to firmly tell my fifteen-year-old daughter, "You're grounded."
>
> She glared at me, and her mouth opened as if she were searching for words. I stood, with my hands on my hips, waiting for the explosion.
>
> To my surprise, her face relaxed. "Good," she said, "cause I'm worn out."
>
> I was stunned. She went into the house, took a quilt and pillow from the closet and returned to the covered front porch. I watched from the doorway as she wrapped up cozily on the cushioned swing.
>
> Her actions calmed me as I looked out at the crisp, autumn day. The only sounds were the rustling of the orange and yellow leaves being shaken from the trees in the gentle breeze and acorns dropping rhythmically onto the roof. Three hours later, she still slept among the autumn splendor.
>
> Her bad attitude made sense to me. She had been exhausted.

When we're physically exhausted, our mental and emotional health suffers too. Our attitude becomes irritable and impatient.

Read Mark 6:31. Depending on the Bible translation you are using, the verbiage may be different, but the concept is the same. Fill in the missing words: *[Jesus said]*, _____ _____ *to a* _____ *and rest a while. For there were many people coming and going, and they [Jesus and the disciples] did not even have time to eat.*

What is the action Jesus said to do?

Where did He suggest they go?

What was happening that prompted His suggestion?

A number of things could've been occurring, but it appears the atmosphere was tense. John the Baptist had been murdered; John's disciples had told Jesus of John's death; the apostles had returned after being sent out to witness (doing church work) and were exhausted. They were so busy they hadn't had time to eat.

Do you think Jesus ever became exhausted? Why or why not?

Jesus said to "come away." What do you think He meant by that? Circle all that apply.

    be still   refocus   refresh   hide
    move away recharge   be tranquil be quiet

What other words come to your mind?

What do you think this means for you today?

When we're too busy, we overlook the joy and beauty of the task at hand. There's not much joy in that. God used my daughter to open my eyes to see my own need for emotional rest. He used the squirrel on its private limb to remind me to slow down, refocus, and be still.

In what ways are you physically or emotionally exhausted?

Ask God for the rest your body needs. Use this verse: *[Jesus says], Come to Me, all you who labor and are heavy laden, and I will give you rest. Take My yoke upon you and learn from Me, for I am gentle and lowly in heart, and you will find rest for your souls.* Matthew 11:28–29 (NKJV)

Notes

In what way do you find that your mind is racing, frantic, or confused?

Ask God to give your mind a rest. Use this verse: *Cease striving and know that I am God; I will be exalted among the nations, I will be exalted in the earth.* Psalm 46:10

Describe how it feels to be worn out emotionally.

Ask God to keep you still if your agenda is hectic. Use this verse: *The Lord will fight for you while you keep silent.* Exodus 14:14 (NIV)

We may not have a choice about some of our activity during a particular season of life. But we do have control over other things. Ask God to show you if there is anything you need to cut from your schedule. To get a visual image, it will help if you see a day in your life written on paper.

Describe a typical day in your life.

Look at your schedule. What things must be done?

What things are optional?

Notes

God will show us each how to manage our individual schedules when we ask Him. In fact, He might even add, "Meet me on the private limb of the tall oak tree!"

What Meant the Most to You from Today's Study?

Application

- Plan a time of rest and relaxation. Schedule it on the calendar, and work hard to protect it. Consider turning off your cell phone and social media. Your time might be thirty minutes, a few hours, a half day, or longer. Do something you like to do — maybe get a pedicure, read a book, sip coffee on the porch and read a psalm, listen to praise music, take a hike, go for a walk, or write in a journal. You're the expert on you! Have fun and be refreshed.

- Listen to "Still" by Hillsong United. https://www.youtube.com/watch?v=z3wwWFsSlNQ

Notes

※

The reasons for busyness range from a temporary situation to a chosen habit. What's important, though, is that we get a sense of what busyness looks like, how it affects us and the people we love, and how we can best deal with it.

※

Light from the Scriptures

Blessed is the man who walks not in the counsel of the wicked, nor stands in the way of sinners, nor sits in the seat of scoffers; but his delight is in the law of the Lord, and on his law he meditates day and night. He is like a tree planted by streams of water that yields its fruit in its season, and its leaf does not wither. In all that he does, he prospers. The wicked are not so, but are like chaff that the wind drives away. Therefore the wicked will not stand in the judgment, nor sinners in the congregation of the righteous; for the Lord knows the way of the righteous, but the way of the wicked will perish.

Psalm 1:1–6 ESV

✼ 25 ✼
Zapped by The Holy Spirit

*The human conscience is reliable
only when it is guided by the Holy Spirit.*

~ Billy Graham

Focus:
We shine when we're controlled by the Holy Spirit.

WHILE WORKING OUTSIDE ON A HOT SUMMER'S DAY, FROM THE corner of my eye, I saw a streak of flesh leaping through the yard. That streak was my six-year-old son running barefoot through the grass in his underwear — with our dog's collar around his neck.

But this was no ordinary collar. We had installed an invisible fence for our dog, Buddy, so the collar Will wore around his neck was an electric collar . . . with a fresh set of batteries.

The collar beeps to alert a dog when he's approaching the boundary. As Buddy gets closer to the border, the collar beeps faster and louder, warning him to stop. If he ignores the beeps and tries to cross the boundary, he receives a mild shock. The shock isn't meant to hurt the dog but to make him uncomfortable enough that he stops and returns to safe territory.

Will was running, collar beeping, as fast as he could toward the border. My husband ran after him and yanked him back just before he would've received an electrical zap.

At that moment, I made a surprising connection: *The Holy Spirit is like my dog's electric collar.*

Just as my family set boundaries to keep Buddy safe, God has established boundaries for His children. And we, like Buddy, also receive warnings to keep us from crossing the border into danger.

To begin with, why do you think God gives us boundaries?

Notes

Notes

Romans 6:23 tells us *the wages of sin is death*. God gives us freedom to choose to live within His boundaries or outside of them. To live outside of God's boundaries means to accept the consequences of destruction and spiritual death. Living inside God's boundaries brings blessings.

God knows that living within His boundaries on our own strength is impossible, so He gave us the Holy Spirit to help.

Read John 14:26. What other names are attached to the Holy Spirit?

Depending on your translation, you may read the words: *Helper, Redeemer, Advocate, Counselor,* or *Comforter*.

While thankful for the Helper, you may wonder, *Does everyone have the Holy Spirit? Every Christian?*

Ephesians 1:13 tells us: *In Him, you also, after listening to the message of truth, the gospel of your salvation – having also believed, you were sealed in Him with the Holy Spirit of promise.*

Recall from chapter one that a seal is a stamp on a package or letter to prove its authenticity as coming from the king. The same applies here: The Holy Spirit shows we belong to God.

When did you accept Jesus as your Savior and receive the Holy Spirit? (If you haven't yet, and would like to, turn to page 258.)

The Bible teaches that the Holy Spirit is the Helper who comes to dwell within us the moment we put our faith in Jesus Christ.

Read John 14:16–17. Where does the Holy Spirit live . . . abide . . . or dwell?

Now turn over a few chapters to John 16:7–8. According to this passage, what does the Holy Spirit do?

Christ followers have been given the Holy Spirit to help us in all areas of life, including helping us heed the warnings of approaching sin and stay within safe boundaries.

Our Helper, the Holy Spirit, Convicts of Sin

Sin creates a wall and separates us from God. But when conviction leads to repentance, we can enjoy a right relationship with Him.

The beeping Will heard was a warning that if he crossed the border, he would receive a shock. Figuratively speaking, how can we avoid being shocked?

While at work one day, I entered a room full of women. Gossip was flying. Something inside me said, "Don't gossip . . . just walk away." I now recognize the "something" as the Holy Spirit nudging me to make the right decision before I became involved.

I refused to take part in the gossip and walked away from the situation. Knowing that gossip is often exchanged in that room, I now avoid that fence by walking in a completely different direction. It's similar to being on a diet and avoiding a room where there's a box of doughnuts. Don't go there.

Notes

Have you worn a path to a particular fence? What is the border you keep coming to?

We don't want to lose the hypothetical collar because it represents the Spirit, who warns us of potentially sinful situations. The inner voice persuades us to stop before we cross the border of sin and receive a full shock — the painful consequence. Many recognize our inner voice as our conscience. But as believers, we know this voice is the Holy Spirit.

Recall a time you clearly felt the Holy Spirit's warning to stop before crossing the border into sin. How did you respond?

What was the outcome?

Had you responded differently, what do you think the outcome would have been?

Turn back to the first page of this chapter and reflect on the question about why God gives us boundaries. What do you think would happen if He didn't give us any boundaries?

Even knowing the consequences, our human nature often prompts us to cross boundaries.

Read Ephesians 4:30 and fill in the missing word: *Do not _____ the Holy Spirit of God, with whom you were sealed for the day of redemption.*

What happens when we ignore the Holy Spirit's promptings?

Most translations use the word *grieve* which means "to cause to suffer, stress, or grief."[80] We grieve the Holy Spirit when we disregard His pleading and disobey. Sin hinders our relationship with God. We're God's children. When we ignore His warnings and give into our sinful desires, He is grieved.

Our Helper, the Holy Spirit, Is a Comforter

Sometimes we stride towards the border where fear, negativity, unfounded guilt, worthlessness, and sadness, are waiting on the other side. When we are approaching this direction, the Holy Spirit corrects our false thinking or lifts us up. He reminds us of God's truth. Read 2 Corinthians 1:3–4. How is God the Father and the Holy Spirit described here?

How has the Holy Spirit comforted you while in an uncomfortable position?

Our Helper, the Holy Spirit, Is Our Teacher and Counselor

Matthew 10:18–20 tells us: *You will even be brought before governors and kings for My sake, as a testimony to them and to the Gentiles. But when they hand you over, do not worry about how or what you are to say; for it will be given you in that hour what you are to say. For it is not you who speak, but it is the Spirit of your Father who speaks in you.*

Circle "for it is not you who speak." The Holy Spirit functions as our teacher.

Notes

When has the Holy Spirit taught you what to say? When has He provided you with a verse or words of encouragement for yourself or someone else at just the right time?

That's another way the Holy Spirit works. He guides us in what to say and do.

Our Helper, the Holy Spirit, Is Powerful

Acts 1:8 tells us: *You will receive _____ when the Holy Spirit comes on you. We receive the Holy Spirit at the time we make Jesus our Savior.*

What comes with the Holy Spirit? _____.

Whew! God does not expect us to live in our own power.

When do you feel powerless against a sinful situation?

We find hope in Galatians 5:16: *Walk by the Spirit, and you will not carry out the desire of the flesh.*

Circle what happens when we walk by/live with the Spirit of God.

First Corinthians 10:13 tells us this: *No temptation has overtaken you but such as is common to man; and God is faithful, who will not allow you to be tempted beyond what you are able, but with the temptation will provide the way of escape also, so that you will be able to endure it.*

Circle what God will provide.

We have the power through Christ. Philippians 4:13 says *I can do _____ through Him who strengthens me.* This includes being victorious over our sinful inclinations.

Our Helper, the Holy Spirit, Intercedes on Our Behalf

Notes

Romans 8:26–27 tells us: *In the same way the Spirit also helps our weakness; for we do not know how to pray as we should, but the Spirit Himself intercedes for us with groanings too deep for words; and He who searches the hearts knows what the mind of the Spirit is, because He intercedes for the saints according to the will of God.*

When we don't know the words to pray, who intercedes for us?

Sometimes, words escape us and all we have to spill are tears. Even then, the Holy Spirit is with us to intervene on our behalf. He is our mighty advocate.

Today we can ask God to help us recognize our inner voice — our conscience — as the voice of the Holy Spirit.

Will is older now. He quit donning Buddy's electrical collar long ago. But when we see any dog safely within the confines of his yard, we can be reminded the Holy Spirit works to keep us safe too. And within this boundary, we'll be a beaming light for others.

What Meant the Most to You from Today's Study?

Notes

> *Sometimes, words escape us and all we have to spill are tears. Even then, the Holy Spirit is with us to intervene on our behalf. He is our mighty advocate.*

Application

➤ We may need reinforcements in an area of our life and need a helping hand from time to time. Think about someone you can reach out to who can help you refrain from taking the path that crosses the border into sin. Identify a godly friend, mentor, or a godly professional counselor who can help you.

➤ Listen to "Holy Spirit" by Kari Jobe.
https://www.youtube.com/watch?v=XPPMSfCdUng

Light from the Scriptures

As it is written: "What no eye has seen, what no ear has heard, and what no human mind has conceived," the things God has prepared for those who love him— these are the things God has revealed to us by his Spirit. The Spirit searches all things, even the deep things of God. For who knows a person's thoughts except their own spirit within them? In the same way no one knows the thoughts of God except the Spirit of God. What we have received is not the spirit of the world, but the Spirit who is from God, so that we may understand what God has freely given us. This is what we speak, not in words taught us by human wisdom but in words taught by the Spirit, explaining spiritual realities with Spirit-taught words. The person without the Spirit does not accept the things that come from the Spirit of God but considers them foolishness, and cannot understand them because they are discerned only through the Spirit. The person with the Spirit makes judgments about all things, but such a person is not subject to merely human judgments, for, "Who has known the mind of the Lord so as to instruct him?" But we have the mind of Christ.

1 Corinthians 2:9–16 NIV

❧ 26 ❧
Spiritual Nourishment

Focus: We shine when we're feasting on God's Word.

*When the child of God looks into the Word of God,
he sees the Son of God.
And he is transformed by the Spirit of God
to share in the glory of God.*

~ Warren Wiersbe

> *My foot has held fast to His path; I have kept His way and not turned aside. I have not departed from the command of His lips; I have treasured the words of His mouth more than necessary food.*
>
> Job 23:11–12

Job treasured God's words and he was spiritually nourished. Imagine . . . God, who spoke creation into existence and gave breath to our body, gives us the Bible so we can live an abundant, meaningful life, enabling us to shine.

The moon on its own would be dark 24/7, but because the moon reflects the light from the sun, we can see it shining brightly. On our own we, too, are dark. But when we study God's Word, we reflect the Light of the World.

The Bible is the world's best-selling and most widely distributed book, with more than five billion copies in print. The full Bible has been translated into 531 languages, and 2,123 languages have a least one book of the Bible translated into that language.[81]

Recall Hebrews 4:12 which says *the word of God is living and active and sharper than any two-edged sword, and piercing as far as the division of soul and spirit, of both joints and marrow, and able to judge the thoughts and intentions of the heart.*

Notes

Based on that verse, is God's Word alive or dead? _____

Alive. Okay . . . but what does that mean? Is the Bible mere paper bound in leather? To articulate the viability and power of the Bible, we can explore synonyms for alive. A quick internet search presents these:

awake	conscious	viable	around	operative
cognizant	dynamic	existing	functioning	subsisting
knowing	living	mortal	working	growing

The Bible contains historical stories, but they aren't outdated. The Bible holds the living words of Almighty God. In this book, God communicates with words that awaken our conscience and enable us to exist.

Refer to Hebrews 4:12. How can the Bible be sharper than a sword — in fact, a two-edged sword?

How can the Bible pierce a heart?

Jeremiah 15:16 says that Jeremiah was spiritually alive — filled with joy — because of the words in the Bible. He said, *Your words were found and I ate them, and Your words became for me a joy and the delight of my heart.*

The Bible sustains life. At the beginning of this chapter we read that Job said he treasured God's words more than food. *Do we?*

Practically speaking, what does food do for our body?

What is the connection between food and God's Word?

Notes

God's Word does for the soul what food does for the human body; it permits us to be spiritually alive and vital.

Read Isaiah 55:11, written here. Then fill in the blanks: *So will My word be which goes forth from My mouth; It will not return to Me empty, without accomplishing what I desire, and without succeeding in the matter for which I sent it.*

God's Word is straight from His _____.

His Word _____ what He desires.

John 6:63 tells us: *It is the Spirit who gives life; the flesh profits nothing; the words that I have spoken to you are spirit and are life.*

Fill in the blank.

God's words are _____.

For our bodies to remain healthy and active, we need:

- water to hydrate and flush out toxins
- minerals to build bones so we can move
- protein to build muscle
- carbohydrates to fuel
- fats to cushion our organs for protection and add flavor[82][83]

Typically, a balanced diet and vitamins provides these things listed.

To stay alive spiritually, we need the Bible to:

- dispel the poisonous, toxic lies of Satan and quench our thirst for truth
- help us move forward and grow
- make us strong and courageous
- energize our spirit
- cushion us against the enemies' attacks.

Some people only reach for the Bible when their world falls apart, just as some people only take vitamins when their body needs to replenish them. But for us to stay spiritually nourished, we need to be filled up regularly with God's words.

Notes

Psalm 34:8 tells us: *O taste and see that the Lord is good; how blessed is the man who takes refuge in Him!*

In this context, *taste* doesn't imply a nibble. Taste means to feed on the Word of God.[84]

Which of these statements best describes you?

- ❏ I nibble on God's Word occasionally.
- ❏ I feed on God's Word regularly.

If you chose nibble, what is the most difficult part about reading the Bible?

If you chose feed, what motivates you to read your Bible regularly?

Just as water hydrates and flushes toxins, God's Word refreshes and reveals truth.

What toxic lie is difficult for you to flush?

Psalm 33:4 tells us: *The word of the Lord is upright.* Identify a verse in Scripture to disprove the devil's lie. It's time to flush the lie and be refreshed.

Just as minerals aid bone strength so we can move, the Bible shows us the direction in which we should move.

In 1 Chronicles 29:19, David prayed for his son Solomon to live by God's Word. Depending on your translation, you will see one of a variety of words: *laws, commands, statutes, decrees, testimonies.*

Remember that statutes are detailed instructions for practical daily living. Commandments are laws or boundaries God gives us to live by.

Read 2 Timothy 3:16–17. What is Scripture profitable for?

_____   _____

_____   _____

God's Word is the prescribed diet that teaches us the right way to live.

Charles Stanley tells us:

> Making Scripture your daily companion is the best way not to miss God's plan. Without significant time in the Word, we tend to forget what matters to God. When we start mixing the world's lies with the Father's truth, we step out of His plan.[85]

In the darkness of night, we cannot see which way to go. Darkness can refer to our state of mind or confusion about our next steps. What is "dark" for you right now?

Ask God to light your lamp and enlighten your darkness (Psalm 18:28).

Recall Psalm 119:105. Imagine you're explaining this verse to a young child. What would you say it means?

Just as protein builds muscle and makes us strong, the Bible gives us the strength and courage for His glory.

In Psalm 72:6 we read this: *May he come down like rain upon the mown grass, like showers that water the earth.* How would you describe what a gentle rain does to hard, cracked, dried-up earth?

Notes

Notes

That's a life-changing impact!

In your own words, on the next page compare God's Word to rain coming down on a hard-hearted, cracked, and dried-up soul. What effect would rain have on your cracked soul?

Read Psalm 1:2–3 and fill in the missing words. Most translations use identical words or synonyms that will fit the blanks.

His delight is in the _____ of the Lord, and on His law he _____ day and night. He is like a _____ planted by streams of _____ which yields its _____ in season and whose leaf does not wither. Whatever he does prospers.

God's Word provides necessary spiritual food and water necessary so we don't wither away.

Just as carbohydrates provide fuel for the body, the Bible energizes our spirit with hope.

Read Psalm 42:11. The Bible teaches that a downcast spirit can be replaced with _____.

Isaiah 40:31 says *those who wait for the Lord will gain new strength; they will mount up with wings like eagles, they will run and not get tired, they will walk and not become weary.*

How do Psalm 42:11 and Isaiah 40:31 energize you?

Just as fats enhance flavor, the Bible flavors life and cushions us with encouragement, joy, and peace.

Psalms 116:2 tells us *because He has inclined His ear to me, therefore I shall call upon Him as long as I live.*

Visualize God cupping His palm around His ear and bending low to hear you. How does this image encourage you?

Read Psalm 40:2. Where was the psalmist?

God lifted him and set his feet where?

Recall a discouraging time. Where did you seek encouragement? Did you find something special in God's Word? If yes, what was it?

Maybe unrest in the country, family, or workplace has robbed you of peace and joy. You can find peace with Jesus' words from John 14:27: *Peace I leave with you; My peace I give to you; not as the world gives do I give to you. Do not let your heart be troubled, nor let it be fearful.*

Maybe now you have a smile on your face. God's words make us spiritually alive and nourish our soul. They:

Refresh the soul
The law of the Lord is perfect, restoring the soul; the testimony of the Lord is sure, making wise the simple. Psalm 19:7

Are better than gold
They are more precious than gold, than much pure gold. Psalm 19:10 NIV

Are sweet
How sweet are Your words to my taste! Yes, sweeter than honey to my mouth! Psalm 119:103

Make us wise
Heed instruction and be wise, and do not neglect it. Proverbs 8:22

Notes

Bring blessing
Blessed are those who hear the word of God and observe it. Luke 11:28

Are true
You are near, O LORD, and all Your commandments are truth. Psalm 119:151

Are perfect
As for God, His way is perfect: The Lord's word is flawless; He shields all who take refuge in Him. Psalm 18:30 NIV

Remain forever
The grass withers, the flower fades, but the word of our God stands forever. Isaiah 40:8

Give understanding
For the LORD gives wisdom; from His mouth come knowledge and understanding. Proverbs 2:6

Lead to successful living
Commit your works to the LORD and your plans will be established. Proverbs 16:3

Are medicine
For they are life to those who find them and health to all their body. Proverbs 4:22

Refuse spiritual starvation and, instead, feast on God's Word in regular Bible-reading. Just as proper nutrition effects the physical development of our body, spiritual food — the nutrient of instruction — transforms. It's impossible to consistently spend time with God and not be changed.

Psalm 119:8 (NIV) tells us *the precepts of the Lord are right, giving joy to the heart. The commands of the Lord are radiant, giving light to the eyes!*

What Meant the Most to You from Today's Study?

Application

➢ Purchase a plant that needs to be watered often. Let taking care of the plant remind you of your own need for daily spiritual nourishment.

➢ If you are new to reading the Word of God, consider using a Bible with footnotes to help you understand what the passage means.

➢ Listen to "Ancient Words" by Michael W. Smith
https://www.youtube.com/watch?v=ouTgX9hcwk4

Light from the Scriptures

But now, O Jacob, listen to the Lord who created you. O Israel, the one who formed you says, "Do not be afraid, for I have ransomed you. I have called you by name; you are mine. When you go through deep waters, I will be with you. When you go through rivers of difficulty, you will not drown. When you walk through the fire of oppression, you will not be burned up; the flames will not consume you. For I am the LORD, your God, the Holy One of Israel, your Savior.

I gave Egypt as a ransom for your freedom; I gave Ethiopia and Seba in your place. Others were given in exchange for you. I traded their lives for yours because you are precious to me. You are honored, and I love you.

Isaiah 43:1–4

Notes

Refuse starvation and instead, feast on God's Word in regular Bible-reading. Just as proper nutrition effects the physical development of the body, spiritual food — the nutrient of instruction — transforms the spirit. It's impossible to consistently spend time with God and not be changed.

Notes

Focus: We shine when we surrender our worries to God.

❦ 27 ❦
When We're Worried

If you believe in a God who controls the big things, you have to believe in a God who controls the little things. It is we, of course, to whom things look "little" or "big."

~ Elisabeth Elliott

> MAMA BIRD FLITTED BETWEEN THE TREES, AS I WATCHED FROM my porch chair one early spring morning. Back and forth she went, all the while tweeting, forewarning her babies she was on her way with succulent grub. I was captivated by the relentless way the mama bird worked at finding food.
>
> I thought about why I was draped in a blanket in my rocking chair on my porch with my Bible and coffee. I needed time alone because I was worried about decisions that needed to be made in the upcoming week.
>
> God knew my heart was heavy. While watching the birds, I was reminded of His relentless love for me and His faithful provision. I knew I'd received a tweet from heaven.
>
> Time to surrender my worries.

We're all prone to worry. It's human nature. Some fight against it. Others wear it like a badge of honor — an indicator of how much they care.

We're wise to remind ourselves of simple, yet profound, truths regarding worry from time to time. Read Matthew 6:25–27 with fresh eyes.

Have you read this passage before? If yes, what effect has this passage had on your life? If not, are you surprised that Jesus tells us not to worry? Why or why not?

Why do you think Jesus included *birds* and worrying in the same parable?

Notes

Why is worry difficult to release?

Depending on the version of the Bible you're reading from, you may have read *anxious* instead of *worry*.

Worry and anxiety can be defined this way:

Worry: To think about problems or fears; to feel or show fear and concern because you think that something bad has happened or could happen.

Anxiety: Fear or nervousness about what might happen.[86]

The Bible Dictionary's definition of worry is "a sense of uneasiness and anxiety about the future. Scripture indicates that such anxiety is ultimately grounded in a lack of trust in God and his purposes."[87]

How is the Bible's definition of worry different from Webster's?

How does the act of worrying indicate a lack of trust in God?

Worry disables faith and immobilizes trust in God; it's a control issue. We don't want to be faithless or be a control freak . . . especially with God. How does *The Bible Dictionary*'s assertion convict you?

Notes

Read Luke 2:41–48, the story of Jesus' journey with His mother and father to the Feast of Passover in Jerusalem.

Describe the scene in Luke 2:43–45.

How many days passed before Mary and Joseph found twelve-year-old Jesus? (v. 46) _____

Where was he found and what was He doing? (vv. 46–47)

How did Jesus' mother respond? (v. 48) Fill in the missing words: *"Son, why have You treated us this way? Behold, Your father and I have been _____ looking for You."*

Depending on your translation, you may have written *anxiously, sorrowing, distressed.*

How does it make you feel knowing that Mary was worried?

Something about Mary's reaction may bring us comfort. Learning that the mother of Jesus — God in flesh — was anxious, worried, distressed, or full of sorrow when Jesus disappeared from the group, comforts us. We've worried, too.

Is it ever okay to worry? We all have concerns and worries. Some are big. Others may be small. Many are life changing. What anxious thought(s) cast a shadow and cover your soul with darkness?

God has given us emotions that enable us to show empathy, love, and compassion. Worry is also an emotion, but of a different kind.

In 1 Peter 5:7 we read these words: *Casting all your anxiety on Him, because He* _____.

Notes

Because God cares for us, He wants to take from us what can adversely affect every area of our life.

R. Leigh Coleman, a reporter with *The Christian Post*, wrote:

> Key features of worry are that it is repetitive and non-productive. Worry can also have negative effects on both your body and your mind. It may cause physical problems such as an upset stomach, headaches, and muscle tension . . . worrying affects our daily life so much that it interferes with the appetite, lifestyle habits, relationships, sleep, and job performance. Many people who worry excessively are so anxiety-ridden that they seek relief in harmful lifestyle habits such as overeating, cigarette smoking, or using alcohol and drugs.

Coleman says to write your worries down on a piece of paper.

> The trick is that whenever you feel plagued by a worrying thought, note it down on a "worry sheet" or a piece of paper next to a desk or bed. Once the worry is written down, forget it and say, "I will worry about that later." This little trick is effective because it bypasses the thought that we have to worry now to fix something. The mind is "fooled" into thinking that it has not given up worrying. Meanwhile, we lose the habit of worrying in the present moment."[88]

King Hezekiah did something similar to writing a "worry sheet" (2 Kings 19). He received the message about the Assyrian army ready to attack Jerusalem. He then took the letter to the temple and laid it before God. King Hezekiah took his worry to God.

Let's return to our previous question. *Is it okay to worry?* _____

Numerous frightful circumstances lead to worry

- A child/loved one is sick.
- Income isn't sufficient to pay bills.
- A marriage is in jeopardy.
- Passing a test is a prerequisite for a job.
- Retirement accounts are lost.
- Justice doesn't prevail in the courtroom.

To "fret" is an action similar to worry. Read Psalms 37:1–8 (NIV).

Notes

Do not fret because of those who are evil or be envious of those who do wrong; for like the grass they will soon wither, like green plants they will soon die away. Trust in the Lord and do good; dwell in the land and enjoy safe pasture. Take delight in the Lord, and he will give you the desires of your heart. Commit your way to the Lord; trust in him and he will do this: He will make your righteous reward shine like the dawn, your vindication like the noonday sun. Be still before the Lord and wait patiently for him; do not fret when people succeed in their ways, when they carry out their wicked schemes. Refrain from anger and turn from wrath; do not fret—it leads only to evil.

Circle the words *do not fret*. How many times in this brief passage are we told do not fret? _____

Instead of fretting, we are commanded to *trust, delight, commit, be still, wait, refrain*. All are verbs indicating an action. Underline each action in the passage. Which action verb is the most difficult for you?

Worry is a knee-jerk reaction that can potentially become a sinful habit. How can worry become a sin?

We may wonder what we can do about our inclination to worry. Let's continue reading Matthew 6:31–33 for the answer.

What are we commanded not to do? (v. 31)

What, instead, must we do? Here's a hint: it begins with "but" (v. 33).

When we immediately turn to God, by *seeking first the kingdom*, we can avoid worry. When we dwell on the thing we're worried about, we cross the border into sin. However, by turning our anxious thoughts to God, we demonstrate in whom we trust. To trust is the opposite of worry.

Recalling the question "what anxious thoughts darken your soul," fill your name in the first blank, your action verb (trust, delight, commit, be still, wait, refrain) on the second blank, and your worry on the last blank.

_____, *do not fret*. _____.
I will help you _____
_____.

Now read *your name, action verb, and your anxious/ worried thoughts*. Read this like God is talking to you. Repeat as often as necessary.

Eighteenth-century preacher and author J. C. Ryle said, "The only way to be really happy in such a world as this, is to be ever casting all our cares on God."[89]

In modern day, we have all kinds of ways to communicate — verbal, texts, and twitter accounts. God is tweeting us to release anything weighing heavy, and instead, focus on Him and His ability to care for us. Worry makes the face sad. But Psalm 34:5 tells us *those who look to Him radiate*.

What Meant the Most to You from Today's Study?

Notes

Application

- When an anxious thought comes, immediately say "Jesus." You may say this several hundred times in a single day.

- When consumed with worry, put on praise music and sing.

- Listen to "Give Me Faith" by Elevation Worship. https://www.youtube.com/watch?v=dNwt7LQiYck

Worry disables faith and immobilizes trust in God; it's a control issue.

Light from the Scriptures

I rejoiced in the Lord greatly, that now at last you have revived your concern for me; indeed, you were concerned before, but you lacked opportunity. Not that I speak from want, for I have learned to be content in whatever circumstances I am. I know how to get along with humble means, and I also know how to live in prosperity; in any and every circumstance I have learned the secret of being filled and going hungry, both of having abundance and suffering need. I can do all things through Him who strengthens me. Nevertheless, you have done well to share with me in my affliction.

Philippians 4:10–14

~ 28 ~
Praise and Thanksgiving, Sacrifice and Joy

Focus:
We shine when we praise and thank God.

Perhaps it takes a purer faith to praise God for unrealized blessings than for those we once enjoyed or those we enjoy now.

~ A. W. Tozer

My mother's cat, her beloved companion and best friend, passed away.

Mom called me, sobbing. She asked my husband and me to come over right away and help her bury the cat in a special place she had prepared in her garden. When we arrived, she placed the cat on a lovely blanket and carried her ever so gently, as if carrying her most precious belonging. She placed the cat on the ground and then prayed.

"Father, I thank You for allowing me to have this cat that brought joy to my life all these years. Praise the Lord!"

I looked into my mom's face. Her eyes were red and wet from tears, but her smile was wide.

My mother knew what it meant to thank God and praise Him in every circumstance. She was able to take the focus off her pain and reflect on God's goodness.

She brought the sacrifice of praise and thanksgiving during a difficult time. For those tender moments her joy exceeded her pain.

Mom had a distinctive way of signing off on her emails to me too. She wrote, "Eternal Praise & Thanksgiving to Almighty God!" I grew accustomed to seeing this. On the day her cat died, though, I wondered what she would say. Would she really praise God? After her declaration, I broke down and wept — not for her cat, but for the way Mom adored and loved God.

King David loved God. David is honored in Scripture because of his habitual praise and thanksgiving to God. There's a

Notes

pattern of praise throughout the psalms David wrote. No matter his circumstances, his roller-coaster emotions, his sin, what his eyes perceived, his rants and doubts, he always came back with praise to the One true God. David knew God was worthy of thanksgiving and would always triumph. When David praised, he focused on God, not himself. His praise brought glory to God and demonstrated faithful obedience. Although he may not have realized it, his praise protected and grounded him — for praise is the bridge to joy.

Joy is a short word, but when a woman is joyful, she's changed in a positive way. Just take a look at synonyms for joy: bubbly, lighthearted, good humored. Joy doesn't necessarily mean feeling happy. Rather, joy is clinging to God's truth and finding contentment in Him despite the circumstances. As a result, a joyful person exudes an optimistic, hopeful attitude. People from all cultures and religions notice this kind of joyful mindset.

Have you ever experienced a hard time, yet you were able to show joy? If so, write about it. If not, what kept you from having joy?

Being joyful doesn't mean we put on an act or that our lives are perfect. Joy results when we focus on God and His attributes.

Recall Psalm 34:5 and fill in the missing word: *Those who look to Him are* _____*!* Most translations use the same word — *radiant*. But the KJV uses "lightened."

How would you describe a radiant person? Would "joyful" be part of your description? Why or why not?

David wrote in Psalm 9:1: *I will give thanks to the L*ORD *with all my heart; I will tell of all Your wonders.* What is David thanking God for?

God is the giver of every good gift; we could spend all day thanking Him for every wonderful gift and deed.

The author of Psalm 113:1–2 wrote: *Praise the Lord! Praise, O servants of the Lord, praise the name of the Lord. Blessed be the name of the Lord from this time forth and forever.*

Both praise and thanksgiving bring attention to God and glorify Him, yet, there's a difference between them, too.

Thanksgiving is

- thanking God for what He's done for you
- thanking God for the specific gifts and blessings He's lavished on you and others — past and present
- expressing gratitude

Praise is

- complimenting God for who He is — His virtues, attributes, and excellence
- admiring God for what He's done apart from what He's done for us personally
- acknowledging His perfection[90]

Researchers R. A. Emmons and M. E. McCullough shared these findings:

> Grateful, optimistic people have more energy, feel more connected to the world, are more spiritually aware, and even have better functioning immune systems. People who are able to see the positive side of their own life tend to describe themselves as happier and more satisfied in general. This holds true regardless of the participants' age, health, or wealth.[91]

Notes

Make two lists:

    I'm thankful for: I praise God for:

Psalm 92:1–5 tells us that thankfulness is good:

*It is good to give thanks to the L*ORD *and to sing praises to Your name, O Most High: to declare Your lovingkindness in the morning and Your faithfulness by night with the ten-stringed lute and with the harp, with resounding music upon the lyre. For You, O L*ORD*, have made me glad by what You have done, I will sing for joy at the works of Your hands. How great are Your works, O L*ORD*! Your thoughts are very deep.*

Circle what the psalmist is thanking and praising God for.

Read Psalm 103:1–5: *Bless the L*ORD*, O my soul, and all that is within me, bless His holy name. Bless the L*ORD*, O my soul, and forget none of His benefits; who pardons all your iniquities, who heals all your diseases; who redeems your life from the pit, who crowns you with lovingkindness and compassion; who satisfies your years with good things, so that your youth is renewed like the eagle.*

This is David's psalm of praise to God for His mercies. What does David credit Him with?

We thank God, and we praise Him too. But what do you think it means to *bless God*?

In these verses, blessing God means praising Him, as in saying, "God, You are so great!"[92]

Generally speaking, when we give thanks for our blessings, are we indicating that we think the blessings are good?

Very often — and this is good — we read on social media the things people are thankful for. People write about vacations, new homes, or answered prayers being a blessing. And they thank God. And again, thanking God is always good.

Have you ever read, though, about a seemingly tough situation — a storm, an unexpected death, a breakup — when the writer thanks God? How can a tough situation also be a blessing?

While on earth we will experience highs and lows — valleys and mountain tops. While we're on the mountaintop, thanksgiving comes easily. But when we're in the valley and our world seems to be caving in around us, giving thanks can be difficult, and, in fact, incomprehensible. This is when thanksgiving is a sacrifice.

Read Psalm 50:23. *He who offers* _____ *of thanksgiving honors Me.*

Most Bible translations say *sacrifice*. Sacrifice is defined as "an act of offering to a deity something precious; something given up or lost."[93]

In the opening story of this chapter, my mother took her focus off of herself and her sadness to praise and thank God. Praise honors God, and sometimes it's a sacrifice we make.

Read 1 Thessalonians 5:18. Circle the statement below that is true:

Give thanks in all circumstances.

Give thanks only when God answers your prayers.

Give thanks only when life is good.

Notes

Notes

Read Hebrews 12:2 to better understand how it's possible to have a thankful heart and be joyful. How was Jesus able to endure the torture at the cross?

The cross in and of itself wasn't a joyful experience; the aftermath was. Jesus kept His focus forward, on the future. He is our example. We have joy when we understand that God is Sovereign and wise and cannot make mistakes.

Reflect on a difficult time in your recent past. Did you feel thankful for your suffering? Explain.

How would you compare *feeling* thankful with *being* thankful?

Feelings are a state of mind — usually based on our surroundings or circumstances — and most of the time they fluctuate. Being thankful is a verb, an action. It's something we do, despite our feelings.

What is most difficult about maintaining an attitude of praise and thanksgiving?

Philippians 2:14 tells us to *do all things without grumbling or disputing*. We can exchange our grumbling with a new thought pattern — that of praise and thanksgiving.

Articulating praise through a tear-stained perspective is difficult, but God has promised to walk alongside us throughout the fiery trial. He will give us the right words to express our praise if we ask.

What hard situation are you currently facing or have you faced recently?

Notes

What is/was hard about giving thanks or praise in this situation?

What are/were you able to praise God for?

What are you learning about God?

What have you learned about God's character that you had never experienced?

During difficult times, we praise God for His faithfulness because He stays by our side. We praise Him for His love and compassion.

Praise and thanksgiving are connected. The woman who praises God thanks Him too. Ultimately, learning to praise God is part of His plan for us.

Psalm 100:4 tells us:
Enter his gates with _____ and his courts with _____; give _____ to him and _____ his name. (NIV)

Like King David, when we institute the habit of sacrificial praise and thanksgiving, we'll radiate joy.

Notes   *What Meant the Most to You from Today's Study?*

> ※
> David is honored in Scripture because of his habitual praise and thanksgiving to God. Throughout the psalms David wrote, there's a pattern of praise. No matter his circumstances, his roller-coaster emotions, his sin, what his eyes perceived, his rants and doubts, he always came back with praise to the One true God.
> ※

Application

- The Psalms are full of praise and thanksgiving. Read one each day. Start with these: Psalm 34, Psalm 96, Psalm 103, Psalm 104, and Psalm 145.

- Read Deborah Presnell's *Shining Through the Psalms*.

- My friend Gloria makes Psalm 100:4 a regular habit. Each day, regardless of her activity, circumstance, or disposition, she has a "Praise Break." During this time, she stops what she's doing and gives praise to God.

- Listen to "Oh Praise the Name" by Hillsong Worship. https://www.youtube.com/watch?v=LqBpifDpNKc

Light from the Scriptures

We urge you, brothers, admonish the idle, encourage the fainthearted, help the weak, be patient with them all. See that no one repays anyone evil for evil, but always seek to do good to one another and to everyone. Rejoice always, pray without ceasing, give thanks in all circumstances; for this is the will of God in Christ Jesus for you. Do not quench the Spirit. Do not despise prophecies, but test everything; hold fast what is good. Abstain from every form of evil. Now may the God of peace himself sanctify you completely, and may your whole spirit and soul and body be kept blameless at the coming of our Lord Jesus Christ. He who calls you is faithful; He will surely do it.

1 Thessalonians 5:14–24 ESV

❦ 29 ❧
God Sees Our Brokenness

I have heard your prayer, I have seen your tears; behold, I will heal you.

2 Kings 20:5

Focus: We shine because God sees our brokenness and heals our heart.

> I ONCE TRIED TO OPEN THE BACK OF A PICTURE FRAME WITH a knife. The end result was a deep cut between my thumb and index finger and a subsequent trip to the emergency room. The doctor stitched me up, and I was home within a few hours, wishing I'd been more patient with that frame.
>
> The stiches held the gash together as the wound healed. Then, at the right time, the stiches were removed.

Stitches serve an important purpose. My external injury and stiches were visible. But there's another kind of injury that's not as obvious — the wounds of the brokenhearted. The Bible tells us in Exodus 15:26, *I am the LORD, your healer*. And Psalm 147:3 says, *He [God] heals the brokenhearted and binds up their wounds*.

In Psalm 147:3, the word translated as *heal* is the Hebrew word *raphe*, which means "to repair and thoroughly make whole; to mend by stitching."[94] The word translated *broken* is the Hebrew *shabar*, which means "to break into pieces."[95] Broken-hearted in this verse means crushed, destroyed or torn.

God mends not only our physical but also our emotional injuries — our shattered, hopeless hearts.

We all can relate to being brokenhearted, crushed, destroyed or torn. Imagine God . . . stitching together our broken hearts.

God sees everything under the sun, including our heartache. He saw Hagar's, too. Hagar is one of the first females we meet in the Bible.

Notes

Hagar may have entered Abram and Sarai's family (later God renamed them Abraham and Sarah) when they left Egypt with Hagar as their slave. In ancient cultures, slavery was a common practice (Genesis 12:20). Between Genesis 12 and 16 we're not told exactly how this family functioned, but we know the family dynamics later became brutal. Read Genesis 16 in its entirety.

Who suggested Abram marry the Egyptian maidservant? (vv. 1–3)

Sarai, who was barren, told Hagar she would be used as a surrogate. As a slave, Hagar had no rights — no choice in the matter and no power to resist.

Although Sarai's request was culturally acceptable, how do you think Hagar felt when told she would be a surrogate?

Verse three tells us Abram took Hagar as his second wife — presumably for the purpose of bearing a child. What can you surmise about how Hagar might have felt?

Do you think Hagar felt used or less than special? Why or why not?

Hagar was a concubine — a wife with a lower status. This may have affected how she responded to Sarai.

What was Hagar's attitude when she became pregnant? (v. 4) Circle all possibilities.

| Prideful | Boastful | Pompous | Quiet |
| Pretentious | Haughty | Embarrassed | Other _____ |

Which of these behaviors were inconsistent with the customary subservient attitude of a maidservant?

What did Sarai tell Abram about Hagar's behavior? (v. 3)

How did Sarai react to Hagar? (v. 6)

Treating another person harshly means that you're treating them excessively critically or negatively; that you are unduly severe in making demands.[96]

What kind of emotional or verbal abuse do you think might have occurred in Abram and Sarai's home?

From the brief description in Genesis 16, we can't discern all that occurred between these two women. We may, however, be familiar with the concealed conflict that might have transpired — beyond the words recorded in Scripture. Whatever happened, a pregnant woman without any family or friends fled to the wilderness. Sounds like the subject of a modern day reality television program: *Real Housewives of Canaan*.

What possible altercations might Hagar and Sarai have had?

What are plausible emotions either woman could have had?

Notes

Why do you think Sarai turned on Hagar and became her bitter rival?

Pregnant and alone — at least, emotionally — Hagar escaped to the wilderness. A few Bible translations replace *wilderness* with *desert*. The two words essentially have the same meaning — a barren, untamed place.

Who saw Hagar in the wilderness? (v. 11)

Just as God questioned Adam and Eve in the garden of Eden (Genesis 3:9), God began with a question for Hagar. What did He ask?

Why do you think God, who already knows everything, questioned Hagar?

What did God say would happen in the future? (v. 11)

Hagar responded with a spot-on observation. She recognized that God saw the magnitude of her pain — complete brokenness and isolation. Then she spoke the words found in Genesis 16:13: ***You are the God who sees me . . . I have now seen the One who sees me.***

The phrase "God who sees me" is *El Roi* in Hebrew. It is only used once in the Bible — right here.[97]

Truth: God saw Hagar. He sees us too.

Psalm 94:7–9 tells us: *They have said, "The Lord does not see, nor does the God of Jacob pay heed." Pay heed, you senseless among the people; and when will you understand, stupid ones? He who planted the ear, does He not hear? He who formed the eye, does He not see?*

Stupidity says God doesn't see. God's Word says He does.

Many of us can relate to being in a desert or wilderness situation. And, like Hagar, we crave an escape from our desperate, helpless state.

Read Psalm 34:18. To whom does the Lord draw near?

What does He ensure for those whose spirit is crushed?

God sees our brokenness and binds up the heart that is shattered.

Unlike the visible stitches in my hand, the stitches God uses are invisible, holding together the wound until the injury is completely mended.

Read Psalm 147:3 again. The Hebrew term for "bind up" is *chabash*. It means to "wrap up our wounds or hurts."[98] Hold that thought, and picture God wrapping a bandage around your pain.

Hagar's life was difficult. She must have felt numerous emotions during the months and years covered so briefly in Scripture:

- Lonely
- Invisible
- Not special
- Frightened
- Broken
- Weary
- Shattered
- Misunderstood
- Other _____

Notes

Notes

When have you experienced these emotions?

Have you ever felt unseen, invisible in the crowd? Describe the situation in a few sentences.

Currently, is there anything you wish you could escape from?

When we pray to El Roi, we're praying to the God who sees everything about us. He knows the number of hairs on our head and every tear we've shed. He sees our hidden pain and the ache of isolation, loss, and emptiness.

Before becoming Abram's second wife, Hagar had already been in a position of weakness as a slave. In her current situation — pregnant and alone — she revisited her weakness, believing she was without hope. Yet God saw Hagar in the wilderness, and His faithfulness to her was refreshing, like a stream of water in a dry place. Sixteen years later and again in a hopeless state, Hagar and her son, Ishmael, were forced to return to the desert. With death imminent, Hagar called out to God. Again, God heard her cries. While Hagar and her son sat dying of thirst, God opened her eyes to see a nearby well (Genesis 21:15–21).

Read John 7:37–39 and fill in the blank. *If anyone is thirsty, let him come to _____ and drink. He who believes in Me, as the Scripture said, 'From his innermost being will flow rivers of living water.'" But this He spoke of the _____, whom those who believed in Him were to receive.*

Sometimes we become dry and thirsty because we've not spent time with God. Other times, we're rigorously serving and ministering to others, and we become drained. Whatever barrenness we're experiencing, the refreshing water is being in the presence of Jesus Christ.

Read Psalm 107:35.

[God] changes a wilderness into a _____.

[God] changes a dry land into _____.

Spiritually speaking, are you in need of a well of refreshing water to sustain you in your dry place?

When our hearts are broken, discouragement can settle in the cracks. We may wonder if God sees the desperate state of our situation or if we're invisible.

Hebrews 4:13 tells us *there is no creature hidden from His sight, but all things are open and laid bare to the eyes of Him with whom we have to do.*

Do you believe God sees you and knows what you're going through? Explain why or why not.

Psalm 34:15 tells us *the eyes of the L{\sc ord} are toward the righteous and His ears are open to their cry.* Do you believe your cries ascend to God's ear? Explain why or why not.

While our vision of our present circumstances is often blurred, God sees with perfect clarity — with His absolute, watchful eye.

In Psalm 139:2–4 we read: *You know when I sit down and when I rise up; You understand my thought from afar. You scrutinize my path and my lying down, and are intimately acquainted with all my ways. Even before there is a word on my tongue, behold, O L{\sc ord}, You know it all.*

According to this passage, what does God know about us — about you in particular?

Notes

God sees your tears and sympathizes with the pain behind them. While I was waiting for my knife-cut wound to heal, I paid attention to how I washed around the gash, being careful not to disturb the stitches. Today, concentrate on what God says about His care for you. Picture Him mending your heart today.

What Meant the Most to You from Today's Study?

> *When we pray to El Roi, we're praying to the God who sees everything about us. He knows the number of hairs on our head and every tear we've shed. He sees our hidden pain and the ache of isolation, loss, and emptiness.*

Application

- Read Chip Ingram's book *Good to Great in God's Eyes*.
- Listen to "The God Who Sees" by Kathie Lee Gifford and Nichole C. Mullen.
  https://www.youtube.com/watch?v=sz81dIfwf4Y

Light from the Scriptures

He will not allow your foot to slip; He who keeps you will not slumber. Behold, He who keeps Israel will neither slumber nor sleep. The LORD is your keeper; The LORD is your shade on your right hand. The sun will not smite you by day, nor the moon by night. The LORD will protect you from all evil; He will keep your soul. The LORD will guard your going out and your coming in from this time forth and forever.

Psalm 121:3–8

๛ 30 ๏
A Shining Legacy

Death is never the last word on the life of a man.
When a man leaves the world, be he righteous or unrighteous,
he leaves something in the world.
He may leave something that will grow and spread
like a cancer or a poison,
or he may leave something like the fragrance of perfume
or a blossom of beauty that permeates the atmosphere with blessing.

~ James Moffatt
Scottish Theologian

Focus:
We continue
to shine
when we leave
a godly legacy.

> MARGARET HUBL MAY NOT HAVE BEEN WELL KNOWN, BUT HER good deeds within her sphere of influence will be remembered for generations. Margaret was a quilter. When she passed away at age 89, the family draped the quilts she had made for her loved ones over the backs of the pews at her funeral service.
> There were dozens!
> Her family reported this was their grandma's way of communicating her love —providing quilts they could wrap up in to stay warm. Her kindness, compassion, generosity, and selfless service to others, is her shining legacy that will never die.[99]

Perhaps it's a strange comparison, but the roots of legacy extend to the olive.

Many of us eat olives — yellow, green, brown, purple, or black. They taste delicious on salads, pizza, pasta, and subs.

The olive has existed and been cultivated by humans for between 5,000–6,000 years. Olive trees can live for centuries, and they remain productive as long as they are pruned correctly. If a tree does die back due to extreme cold, its roots can survive and produce new shoots.

Notes

Some olive trees in the groves around the Mediterranean have lived as long as 2,000 years. One tree on the island of Brijuni, Croatia, is about 1,600 years old and still bears fruit that is made into top quality olive oil.[100, 101]

Can you imagine the olive trees in the Garden of Gethsemane? They date back to the time of Jesus.

The psalmist tells us this in Psalm 52:8: *As for me, I am like a green olive tree in the house of God; I trust in the lovingkindness of God forever and ever.*

Of all the things to compare oneself to, an olive doesn't seem like an obvious option — not at first anyway.

To be likened to something means to have the attributes of that object.

When we're in a right relationship with God, we strive to demonstrate eight attributes associated with the unique olive tree.

1. **Regardless of its surrounding — hot, dry, cold, wet, rocky, sand — the olive tree survives and thrives.**

Although the branches and trunk might die, the roots never do. Because the roots never die, the olive tree symbolizes faithfulness, perseverance, steadfastness, stability, and endurance.

Perseverance is continued effort to do or achieve something despite difficulties, failure, or opposition; steadfastness.

Steadfastness is similar in definition to perseverance: "Firmly fixed, not subject to change; a firm belief, determination, or allegiance."[103] The implication for Christ-followers is that we remain steady while seeking God's will; we persevere through crushing circumstances.

Identify your current crushing circumstance. In what ways can you demonstrate steadfastness?

Recall David's prayer in Psalm 51:10: *Create in me a clean heart, O God, and renew a steadfast spirit within me.*

When David asks God to renew a steadfast spirit, what does he want God to do?

God answered David's prayer. In Psalm 57:7 David wrote, *My heart is steadfast, O God, my heart is steadfast; I will sing, yes, I will sing praises!*

God enables us to be steadfast. Take a break and say or write a prayer. Ask God to help you be steadfast.

Hebrews 10:36 tells us: *You have need of endurance, so that when you have done the will of God, you may receive what was promised.*

When you are ready to give up, ask God for endurance to finish strong.

2. Olive tree blooms produce a sweet fragrance.

This may be a strange question to ask ourselves, but what do we smell like? Second Corinthians 2:15 tells us *we are a fragrance of Christ to God among those who are being saved and among those who are perishing.*

The *Thomas Nelson Personal Study Bible* notes explain that spreading the gospel of Jesus Christ is a fragrance that rises up to God. Those who reject the gospel bring the smell of death. But to those who accept the gospel release the fragrance of life. As Paul spread the love of Jesus, he left a fragrance — a metaphor for spreading the scent of Christ.[103]

The roots of the faithful will produce a new tree with fragrant blooms. Back to that initial thought: How would you describe your current fragrance?

What needs to die in your life so that you can be a sweet-smelling aroma to those around you?

The more we become like Christ the more we become the fragrance of new life.

3. The oil and leaves from the olive branch are medicinal and bring healing.

Olive leaves can help lower bad cholesterol and blood pressure and help guard against cognitive decline. Just as olive oil promotes health, our words promote healing to the weary soul — words that inspire and encourage. Recall Proverbs 18:21: *Death and life are in the power of the tongue.*

To whom can you speak life-giving, healing words today?

When has someone used words to bring healing to your life?

What, if anything, did it prompt you to do?

4. In ancient times, it was common for the oil of crushed olives to be used for soap.

Soap is used to cleanse and purify. The ancient Greeks smeared olive oil on their hair for grooming purposes. They rubbed olive oil on their bodies for general good health.

Soap made of pure olive oil is still being produced today. Soap cleanses the external body, but what cleanses our spirit?

First Peter 1:2 tells us that the Holy Spirit cleanses us. Christ in us, symbolized by the olive oil, sanctifies our lives and makes us holy.[104] Our word *sanctification* comes from the Greek word *hagiosmo*, and means "set apart" for God's purpose.[105]

Go back to the first attribute of olive oil and reread Psalm 51:10. What did the psalmist want God to clean?

Are you clean? Ask God to show you any area of your life that needs to be washed.

When God sanctifies us, we become "set apart" and able to reflect Jesus and do God's will. In what ways are you "set apart" to reflect Jesus in your ordinary day?

5. Ripe olive fruit taste good.

Like olives, salt enhances the taste of our food.

In Matthew 5:13 Jesus said, *"You are the salt of the earth; but if the salt has become tasteless, how can it be made salty again? It is no longer good for anything, except to be thrown out and trampled under foot by men."*

Jesus compared believers to salt to demonstrate our potential to flavor, preserve, and enhance another person's life. But if salt is abused, it can be harmful. And if salt is diluted by water, it becomes useless.

In the same manner, if Christ-followers become diluted, we're ineffective in flavoring the world.

How does the acceptance of a secular worldview dilute God's truth?

What can we do to keep from being diluted?

Notes

What are some ways you enjoy "flavoring" those around you?

6. Olive wood is durable and colorful. It also has interesting grain patterns.

Olive wood serves a purpose. Because the tree is small and slow growing, its relatively expensive exotic wood is valued by woodworkers. Carved wooden bowls, cooking utensils, cutting boards, fine furniture, and decorative items are made from olive wood.

Likewise, we're extraordinarily valued by God, created *on purpose and with a purpose.* Refresh yourself by rereading Jeremiah 29:11 written here: *I know the plans I have for you, declares the Lord, plans to prosper you and not to harm you, plans to give you hope and a future.* (NIV)

What do you believe your purpose is today?

In what ways are you being prepared today for your next season of life?

7. The olive tree symbolizes productivity, vitality, and long life.

Vitality can be defined as "life; the ability to last." Olive tree roots don't die — and neither do ours. Our roots (thus, our fruit) are our legacy. What we do in our lifetime is what we leave behind. James Moffatt said, "Death is never the last word." What does your life symbolize? What legacy are you leaving? What legacy would you like to leave?

8. **Olive oil is used to fuel lamps.**

You and I are commissioned to light the world. Read Matthew 5:14–16 written here:

You are the light of the world. A city set on a hill cannot be hidden; nor does anyone light a lamp and put it under a basket, but on the lampstand, and it gives light to all who are in the house. Let your light shine before men in such a way that they may see your good works, and glorify your Father who is in heaven.

You are a light. Are you hidden or are you visible?

Describe how you light up a room in each of the following settings. If you don't currently shine, how would you like to?

Work

Church

Home

Community

We're not left to shine on our own. Recall Psalm 18:28. Who keeps our lamps burning?

Notes

When we feel our light going dim, God will reach down and light our fire.

Yes, like the olive tree roots, we'll never die. We'll leave a legacy for future generations.

Just one more time . . .

Let your light shine before men in such a way that they may see your good works, and glorify your Father who is in heaven. Matthew 5:16

What Meant the Most to You from Today's Study?

Application

- ➢ Host a pizza party (or another meal with olives) and teach the eight truths you've just learned. There's no minimum or maximum age on this one. Small children, teens, and adults can all make personal application that is age appropriate and relevant.

- ➢ Listen to "Well Done" by the Afters. https://www.youtube.com/watch?v=lZu7mfYS_VY

Light from the Scriptures

I heard a loud voice from the throne, saying, "Behold, the tabernacle of God is among men, and He will dwell among them, and they shall be His people, and God Himself will be among them, and He will wipe away every tear from their eyes; and there will no longer be any death; there will no longer be any mourning, or crying, or pain; the first things have passed away." And He who sits on the throne said, "Behold, I am making all things new." And He said, "Write, for these words are faithful and true." Then He said to me, "It is done. I am the Alpha and the Omega, the beginning and the end. I will give to the one who thirsts from the spring of the water of life without cost. He who overcomes will inherit these things, and I will be his God and he will be My son.

Revelation 21:3-7

Notes

⋊⋉
When God sanctifies us, we become "set apart" and able to reflect Jesus and do God's will.
⋊⋉

Notes

How to Make a Decision for Jesus

The most important decision you will ever make has nothing to do with other people or anything on this earth. It doesn't even have anything to do with organized religion or a specific denomination. The most important decision you'll ever make is whether to have a personal relationship with Jesus Christ — a decision that will give you peace knowing you will spend eternity in heaven with God.

God's way is simple. We don't have to clean up our lives. We come to God as we are and He cleans us up.

God is holy and cannot look upon sin. So out of His great love, compassion, and mercy for all of humanity, God made a way for us to be in right relationship with Him. He sent His Son, Jesus, to be the sacrifice and die on a cross for us.

John 3:16 tells us *God so loved the world that He gave His only Son that whosoever believes in Him will not perish but have everlasting life*.

Admit you are a sinner. Ask God's forgiveness. Believe that Jesus died on the cross and three days later rose from death to life. Ask Him to be your Savior and take control of your life.

God has a beautiful plan and purpose for you.

You may find it easier to use this prayer:

> "God, I know I am a sinner. I'm sorry for my sins, and I ask Your forgiveness. I believe that You sent Your Son, Jesus Christ, as a sacrifice and that He died and rose again. I invite You into my life. I give You control. Thank You for saving me. I know that I will spend eternity with You. In Jesus' name, amen."

If you prayed this prayer, please let someone know. You can email me at debpres@yahoo.com. Attend a Bible-believing church and cultivate this new, amazing relationship with God.

About the Author

Debbie Presnell, whose career has spanned more than three decades of teaching — from elementary school to higher education, where she trained future teachers — is a member of Gardner-Webb University's Gallery of Distinguished Alumni, a published author, national speaker, and Bible study teacher. She is also a national spokesperson for Mukti Mission in India where she partners with Mukti Mission US to bring hope, healing, and life to women and children of India.

Debbie is called to inspire women and feels honored when God allows her the opportunity to share at women's events about His faithfulness. For the past 25 years, she has spoken at teacher conferences and universities, where she shines the light on her favorite topic: "The Inspirational Classroom: A Guide for Teachers in All School Environments." This will be the subject of an upcoming book. Debbie's first book, *Shine! Radiating the Love of God — A Bible Study for Young Women in Middle School and High School*, is used in her popular Shine Camp. Her devotional is *Shining Through the Psalms — A 150–Day Devotional Journey*. Her books are available on Amazon.com. Additionally, her articles have been published in the *Divine Moments* series compiled by Yvonne Lehman.

Debbie blogs and posts inspirational messages on her Facebook page: ShineEveryDayNC. She and her husband, Alan, have three adult children, a ten-year-old granddaughter, and one baby grandson. She enjoys camping, riding her bike, helping coach a girl's running team, and she loves both the mountains and the beach. When she's not busy writing or speaking, she serves as a substitute teacher in her local school districts. But her best day is Sunday when her entire family gathers for lunch. Visit her website at www.debbiepresnell.com. Email her at debpres@yahoo.com for information about having her speak to your group.

Special Thanks

Thank You, God, for Your lessons. Thank You for Your love and compassion, forgiveness and mercy. Most of all, thank You for your sacrifice — my free gift of salvation.

Thank you, Blue Ridge Christian Writers Critique Group for your valuable input. You labored with me . . . to produce a Bible study that brings glory to God.

Thank you, Denise Loock, for your expert editing services. You "clean me up" real nice.

Thank you to all the wonderful ladies who studied each chapter while it was being written. You're an amazing test group.

Thank you, Meg. You read and studied. You gave countless hours of encouragement. Your insight into every chapter blessed both of us.

Finally, thank you to my publisher, Terri Kalfas, who believes in me.

Notes

Endnotes

1. christiancourier.com/articles/305-lord-and-lord-whats-the-difference
2. *Merriam-Webster's Online Dictionary*, copyright © 2015 by Merriam-Webster, Incorporated/atonement
3. npr.org/sections/krulwich/2012/09/17/161096233/whichis-greater-the-number-of-sand-grains-on-earth-or-stars-in-the-sky
4. dictionary.com/browse/adopt
5. *Webster's Online*
6. Charles Stanley, *In Touch Magazine*, InTouch Ministries, Atlanta Georgia; Sept. 2017, p. 5.
7. *Webster's Online*
8. dictionary.com/browse/disappointment
9. psychologytoday.com/blog/beyond-words/201109/is-nonverbal-communication-numbers-game
10. livescience.com/20578-social-connection-smile-strangers.html
11. goodreads.com/quotes/936465-the-gospel-prayer-in-christ-there-is-nothing-i-can
12. artofmanliness.com/2012/02/05/look-em-in-the-eye-part-i-the-importance-of-eye-contact/
13. *Webster's Online*
14. https://www.pewforum.org/2019/10/17/in-u-s-decline-of-christianity-continues-at-rapid-pace/
15. Thomas E. Trask and Wade I. Goodall, *The Fruit of the Spirit*, Zondervan, 2000, 81.
16. http://www.biblestudytools.com/dictionary/walk/
17. https://www.allchristianquotes.org/authors/ CS Lewis
18. Trask and Goodall, 164; quote from Carl Linquist, "Issues of the Church," Quoted in Larson, Illustrations, 17.
19. biblestudytools.com/lexicons/greek/nas/purosis.html
20. biblehub.com/greek/3986.htm-Peirasmos;
21. biblehub.com/greek/1383.htm-Dokimion
22. dictionary.com/browse/hope
23. biblestudytools.com/dictionary/hope/
24. *Webster's Online*
25. en.wikipedia.org/wiki/Hannah_More
26. womeninscripture.com/2013/11/06/the-pharaohs-daughter-moses-adoptive-mother/
27. *Webster's Online*
28. Ibid.
29. desiringgod.org/messages/how-the-spirit-helps-us-understand
30. intouch.org/read/magazine/daily-devotions/the-need-for-friendship- July 2015
31. *Webster's Online*
32. *The Nelson's NKJV Study Bible*, note on Proverbs 18:24
33. biblehub.com/commentaries/proverbs/18-24.htm-Gills commentary

Notes

[34] gotquestions.org/Bible-trust.html
[35] *Webster's Online*
[36] huffingtonpost.com/dr-cynthia-thaik/emotional-wellness_b_4612392.html
[37] Max Anders, *Thirty Days to Understanding the Bible*, Thomas Nelson, 2004, 57.
[38] *Webster's Online*
[39] compellingtruth.org/holy-holy-holy.html
[40] Ibid
[41] biblestudytools.com/dictionary/fast-fasting/
[42] *Webster's Online*
[43] *The NKJV Personal Study Bible*, Thomas Nelson, 1549, Focus Notes for Pharisee and Scribe.
[44] biblehub.com/greek/3759.htm, meaning of woe.
[45] biography.com/activist/anne-sullivan
[46] phrases.org.uk/meanings/sticks-and-stones-may-break-my-bones.html
[47] *Webster's Online*
[48] biblehub.com/greek/1228.htm
[49] Duncan, J.T. *Owls of the World: Their Lives, Behavior, and Survival,* Firefly Books, 2003.
[50] thefreedictionary.com/wisdom and knowledge
[51] biblehub.com/greek/4678.htmWisdom- Greek word sophias
[52] Warren W. Wiersbe, *Be Mature*, David C. Cook, 2008, 111.
[53] goodreads.com/quotes/29559-wisdom-is-the-right-use-of-knowledge-to-know-is
[54] *The New King James Version Thomas Nelson Study Bible*, Introduction to the Proverbs, 902-903
[55] dailymail.co.uk/femail/article-3029777/Dove-survey-reveals-96-CENT-women-rate-average- looking.html
[56] *Webster's Online*
[57] biblestudytools.com/commentaries/treasury-of-david/ psalms-144-12.html
[58] Ibid
[59] biblestudytools.com/commentaries/treasury-of-david/psalms-45-13.html
[60] drleaf.com/blog/you-are-what-you-think-75-98-of-mental-and-physical-illnesses-come-from-our-thought-life/
[61] en.wikipedia.org/wiki/Fountain_of_Youth
[62] *Webster's Online*
[63] biblehub.com/hebrew/2318.htm
[64] biblehub.com/commentaries/2_timothy/1-7.htm (Barnes Commentary)
[65] greekwordstudies.blogspot.com/2007/04/guard.html /Strong's Number: 5432
[66] *Webster's Online*
[67] Ibid
[68] christianquotes.info/top-quotes/16-wise-christian-quotes-by-augustine/#axzz4oMZPPYMU
[69] biblehub.com/commentaries/deuteronomy/30-12.htm
[70] vocabulary.com dictionary
[71] *Webster's Online*
[72] biblehub.com/commentaries/2_timothy/4-2.htm
[73] gospelhall.org/bible/bible.php?passage=2%20Timothy+4&ver1=kjv&commentary=jamison
[74] biblestudytools.com/lexicons/greek/nas/parakaleo.html
[75] en.oxforddictionaries.com/definition/activity/busyness
[76] hbr.org/2016/12/research-why-americans-are-so-impressed-by-busyness (by Silvia Bellezza, Neeru Paharia, Anat Keinan)
[77] focusonthefamily.com/about/focus-findings/parenting/why-is-mom-too-busy
[78] biblehub.com/luke/10-41.htm- Gill's Exposition & Elliott's commentary
[79] dailytelegraph.com.au/newslocal/news/how-to-be-the-boss-of-busy/newsstory/90345ec8c70f2b2d5de2beda8aadd183

Notes

80 *Webster's Online*
81 guinnessworldrecords.com/world-records/best-selling-book-of-non-fiction/
82 healthyeating.sfgate.com/food-provide-human-body-6194.html
83 cyh.com/HealthTopics/HealthTopicDetailsKids.aspx?p=335&np=284&id=1431
84 Wiersbe, *Be Worshipful*. David C Cook, 2009, 129.
85 Stanley, *In Touch Magazine*, InTouch Ministries, Atlanta Georgia; May 2013. Daily Devotions from The Sermons of Charles Stanley — Day 22, page 53.
86 *Webster's Online*
87 biblegateway.com/resources/dictionary-of-bible-themes/8849-worry
88 christianpost.com/news/are-you-a-worry-wart-52589/June 20, 2011
89 azquotes.com/author/17287-J_C_Ryle
90 differencebetween.com/difference-between-praise-and-vs-thanksgiving/
91 R.A. Emmons and M.E. McCullough, "Counting blessings verses burdens: Experimental studies of gratitude and subjective well-being in daily life," *Journal of Personality and Social Psychology* 84, no.2 (2003): 377-89.
92 desiringgod.org/articles/what-does-it-mean-to-bless-god- John Piper
93 Webster Online
94 bibleapps.com/hebrew/7495.htm
95 bibletools.org/index.cfm/fuseaction/Lexicon.show/ID/H7665/shabar.htm
96 Webster's Online
97 biblehub.com/hebrew/7210.htm
98 biblehub.com/hebrew/2280.htm
99 www.today.com/news/family-honors-grandma-s-memory-displaying-all-her-quilts-her-t108586
100 en.wikipedia.org/wiki/Olive
101 lifeextension.com/magazine/2013/6/unexpected-benefits
102 Webster Online
103 *Thomas Nelson Personal Study Bible* notes; 2 Cor. 2:15
104 Patterson and Kelly, *Women's Evangelical Commentary-New Testament*. Broadman and Holman 2006, 471 & 812- 1 Peter 1:2
105 biblestudytools.com/dictionary/sanctification

Milton Keynes UK
Ingram Content Group UK Ltd.
UKHW052224040923
428043UK00010B/1151